2004

Socrates Meets Machiavelli

Socrates Meets Machiavelli

The Father of Philosophy
Cross-Examines the
Author of *The Prince*

by Peter Kreeft

IGNATIUS PRESS   SAN FRANCISCO

The author expresses his appreciation for permission to reprint excerpts from

The Prince, translated with an introduction by George Bull (Harmondsworth, England, and New York: Penguin Books, 1975).

The Prince: with Selections from The Discourses, translated by Daniel Donno, edited and with an introduction by the translator (Toronto and New York: Bantam Classic, 1981).

Machiavelli, *Selected Political Writings*, translated by David Wootton (Indianapolis: Hackett Publishing, 1994.) Reprinted by permission of Hackett Publishing Company, Inc. All rights reserved.

Cover art: Stone Head of Socrates (469–399 B.C.)
(classic sculpture)
The Louvre, Paris, France / Bridgeman Art Library

Cover design by Roxanne Mei Lum

ISBN 0–89870–926–1
Library of Congress Control Number 2001098030
Printed in the United States of America ∞

Contents

5

Introduction

This book is one in a series of Socratic explorations of some of the Great Books. Books in this series are intended to be short, clear, and non-technical, thus fully understandable by beginners. They also introduce (or review) the basic questions in the fundamental divisions of philosophy (see the chapter titles): metaphysics, epistemology, anthropology, ethics, logic, and method. They are designed both for classroom use and for educational do-it-yourselfers.

The "Socrates Meets . . ." books can be read and understood completely on their own, but each is best appreciated after reading the little classic it engages in dialogue.

The setting—Socrates and the author of the Great Book meeting in the afterlife—need not deter readers who do not believe there is an afterlife. For although the two characters and their philosophies are historically real, their conversation, of course, is not and requires a "willing suspension of disbelief". There is no reason the skeptic cannot extend this literary belief also to the setting.

I

The Characters

SOCRATES: Here! Here, Niccolò, over here.

MACHIAVELLI: Who—what—where? Who are you, sir, that you dare to call me like a dog? Show yourself!

SOCRATES: I am right here, directly in front of you.

MACHIAVELLI: Well, I can't see you through all this damned fog. Where the Hell am I?

SOCRATES: Fear not, you are not in Hell.

MACHIAVELLI: I didn't mean it literally, you simpleton!

SOCRATES: Are you sure? Was that not your deepest fear?

MACHIAVELLI: I was not so dogmatic as to claim knowledge of the next world, like all those credulous Christians.

SOCRATES: And therefore you had no fear of what might await you? You did *not* claim to know that "all those credulous Christians" were *right* about there being an afterlife and a Hell; did you claim to know that they were *wrong*?

9

MACHIAVELLI: I was a practical person. Correction: I *am* a practical person. (Why am I speaking of myself as if I were dead?)

SOCRATES: If you were a practical person, why did you not take measures against this feared and unknown future when you had the power to do so? Did this not contradict one of the most practical principles in your own book?

MACHIAVELLI: You've read my book?

SOCRATES: I have.

MACHIAVELLI: And—?

SOCRATES: I admire your practical wisdom in many places. For instance—let's see—I know I remember the place—

MACHIAVELLI: You have my book there! I can see you now—why is there still this fog?

SOCRATES: The fog is only in your mind, my friend, as you will soon see. That's one of the peculiarities of this place. Ah, yes, here's the passage, I knew it was there in chapter 3, where you go on about the Romans, your heroes of practical wisdom: I quote—

MACHIAVELLI: Wait! Who are you? And why do you have my book with you? And what is this place?

SOCRATES: All in good time, my friend, all in good time. I will not be distracted from this point, this wonderfully wise passage—

MACHIAVELLI: You want to prove to me that I should have had the fear of Hell—from my own words?

SOCRATES: Exactly.

MACHIAVELLI: Are you from the Inquisition?

SOCRATES: Oh, my, no! Nothing like that *here*. And yet, in a sense, you may say that I am a one-man inquisition. Inquiry, now, that's my thing. But none of those ridiculous threats of torture. No, no, I will not be distracted. Where's that passage? I've lost it again—

MACHIAVELLI: The middle of chapter 3. In the paragraph beginning with "The Romans".

SOCRATES: Thank you. Yes, there it is. You are wise to know exactly what I was going to read.

MACHIAVELLI: Then why waste time reading it?

SOCRATES: Oh, no time can be wasted here.

MACHIAVELLI: Here?

SOCRATES: For the last time, no more distractions! Here—

MACHIAVELLI: I hate that word!

SOCRATES: Listen to this:

> **[T]he Romans did what all wise rulers must: cope not only with present troubles but also with ones likely to arise in future, and assiduously forestall them. When trouble is sensed well in advance it can easily be remedied; if you wait for it to show itself any medicine will be too late because the disease will have become incurable. As the doctors say of a wasting disease, to start with it is easy to cure**

but difficult to diagnose; after a time, unless it has been diagnosed and treated at the outset, it becomes easy to diagnose but difficult to cure. So it is in politics.

Bull p. 39,
ll. 20–30.

You knew this principle in regard to the body and the body politic; why did you not know it in regard to your soul?

MACHIAVELLI: Now I can see you—

SOCRATES: You must answer the question, you know, either sooner or later. There's no more hiding here.

MACHIAVELLI: You said that "here" is not Hell.

SOCRATES: Correct.

MACHIAVELLI: I did die, didn't I?

SOCRATES: Correct again.

MACHIAVELLI: So is this Heaven or Purgatory?

SOCRATES: It is Purgatory for you and Heaven for me.

MACHIAVELLI: How can that be?

SOCRATES: It is for me a continuation of the most heavenly task I knew on earth: to inquire of the great sages, to pursue wisdom from those who know. For they are the opposite of myself, who do not know. And it will be Purgatory for you as it was to my fellow citizens on earth. But here no one has power to give the gadfly a swat and send him away to the next world. This *is* the next world. You must endure my questions.

MACHIAVELLI: So you *are* my torturer.

SOCRATES: No, I am your friend.

MACHIAVELLI: My inquisitor.

SOCRATES: No, your teacher.

MACHIAVELLI: By means of inquisition.

SOCRATES: No, by means of inquiry. The unexamined life is not worth living, you know.

MACHIAVELLI: Now I see clearly, you ugly old man. I know who you are.

SOCRATES: I thought that would be obvious.

MACHIAVELLI: You're one of those Socrates impersonators. I've seen a dozen of you at the university. You're tediously unoriginal.

SOCRATES: I guess it's not so obvious after all. No, Niccolò, I am the genuine article, the original, I assure you.

MACHIAVELLI: So this is my Purgatory: to be cross-examined by Socrates.

SOCRATES: I'm afraid so.

MACHIAVELLI: Do I have any alternatives? Any choice?

SOCRATES: No. We both have to fulfill our orders. They come from higher authority. You see, every philosopher has to endure my questions. You are not alone.

MACHIAVELLI: Plato, too? Did Plato have to face you?

SOCRATES: Indeed, he did.

MACHIAVELLI: How I would love to hear that exchange!

SOCRATES: It is not permitted. Not now, anyway. Perhaps later, much later. But now it would be a distraction. And that is exactly the opposite of what this place is for.

MACHIAVELLI: Must I answer to you for everything?

SOCRATES: Oh, my goodness, no! Only your work, not your life. And only your writing, not your other work. And only *The Prince*.

MACHIAVELLI: My masterpiece.

SOCRATES: That remains to be seen. I will tell you, however, that your book was one of the most influential ever written. Even though almost no one totally agreed with you, everyone was influenced by you. You have been called the father of modern political philosophy.

MACHIAVELLI: Ha! They said they didn't agree with me; but secretly they knew I spoke the truth—otherwise they would not have used me so fundamentally that I could be called "the father of modern political philosophy". That is what you said, isn't it?

SOCRATES: Yes, but—

MACHIAVELLI: I like that title. I like it very much. Now I see why they sent you to meet me. You are the real thing, aren't you?

SOCRATES: Do I look like a Coke bottle?

MACHIAVELLI: A *what*?

SOCRATES: A feeble jest. You will understand it later. (In fact, I do look remarkably like a Coke bottle.)

"The real thing", you say: I wonder what you mean by that?

MACHIAVELLI: Ah, now I know you are indeed the real thing, Socrates; I recognize your fingerprint, your almost addictive desire for definitions. So this *is* the next world! Ah—look here, Socrates, I'm going to make you an offer you can't refuse. Employ me! Make me your partner here. I have just what you need for this job: the extensive knowledge of real life, not just ideas, and real human beings, not just ideal human nature. I have much experience, and I have studied history.

SOCRATES: You have a very clever sense of humor, Niccolò.

MACHIAVELLI: I am totally serious, Socrates. I realize what this situation looks like from your point of view. You have the power, and you wonder what I could possibly offer you.

Well, Socrates, I know you will agree that understanding is the most valuable thing in the world; and I have never found among all my possessions anything that I hold more dear than my understanding of the deeds of great men—as you must know if you have read my book. So I hope it will not be presumptuous for a man of low and humble status to advise you, O great Socrates, the wisest man in the world. For those in low valleys have a perspective on mountaintops and those who dwell on them that those dwellers do not and cannot have. You have climbed to the mountaintop of wisdom, leaving the mass of men back in the cave. For this very reason, I, who have made it my lifelong task to explore the cave, can teach you about men who dwell there and about how they fight about shadows. You know the true good, but I know more about falsehood and lies and evil. And if, in your heavenly wisdom, you look down to the realms of darkness in which I have lived, you will understand that I am truly an expert on the subject of evil fortune.

SOCRATES: You *are* serious, aren't you?

MACHIAVELLI: Absolutely. Employ me, Socrates. What a combination we would make! I'm making you an offer you can't refuse.

SOCRATES: You're not acting?

MACHIAVELLI: No, why do you keep asking that?

SOCRATES: Because you are parodying yourself. Have you forgotten what you wrote in the dedicatory letter to Lorenzo the Magnificent that you put at the beginning of your book? You used the same argument, even the same imagery, to persuade him to employ you—and the same shameless flattery and insult—

MACHIAVELLI: Insult? No! Not to you!

SOCRATES: You devoted a whole chapter of *The Prince* to the subject of flatterers: **"How Sycophants Are to Be Shunned"**. And you sent the book to Lorenzo as a job application with a cover letter of shameless flattery! You must have thought the mind of Lorenzo the Magnificent to be something less than magnificent. And mine as well, if you thought I would not see that contradiction.

MACHIAVELLI: You have no peer in that, Socrates. Spotting contradictions is to you what finding ants is to an anteater.

SOCRATES: Well at least we have left the realm of flattery . . .

MACHIAVELLI: Will you open your mind to my proposal?

SOCRATES: Even if I were tempted to consider it—which I am not—it is impossible. It is forbidden. We two have another task to perform here, and you are not my co-examiner but my examinee.

MACHIAVELLI: Ah, I understand. I would not dream of opposing your Masters' will. By the way, *you* have never considered that option, have you? Just as a thought experiment, of course. I think you are interested in all thought experiments. Perhaps you could use my experience and expertise to explore what is possibly the only thought experiment you have never explored—

SOCRATES: Stop! Hush! Do you think I am as naïve as the woman in the garden? Or—to speak in terms of *your* categories—who do you think holds the power here?

MACHIAVELLI: You misunderstand my intention.

SOCRATES: I cannot know intentions. There is, however, One who can. So I would strongly suggest avoiding dallying with that "thought experiment", even for one second. For though you may indeed deceive me, I am not in charge here. I think you know who is.

MACHIAVELLI: I shall be as pious as a sheep. What must I do to be saved?

SOCRATES: (Even now the fool toys with the fire!) Many things, my friend, but for now, only one preliminary thing: you must "know thyself". That is why I was sent to you. I shall hold up your own book to be a mirror.

MACHIAVELLI: You will correct me?

SOCRATES: No, I will question you, and you will answer; and, if you will, you shall correct yourself.

MACHIAVELLI: Of course. Your famous "Socratic method". Well, since it seems I have no choice, proceed.

SOCRATES: You *have* a choice. That is what a question is: a choice. Two roads open out, at least, after every question: yes and no. And it is your choice alone that will determine the path you take. I know you must understand because you have read Plato's accounts of the questions I asked some of my fellow citizens in Athens, and you are a very intelligent man.

MACHIAVELLI: You know me well, Socrates. Let us proceed.

2

The Contrast with Plato

SOCRATES: Where do you prefer to begin?

MACHIAVELLI: At the beginning.

SOCRATES: A wise choice. I take it you mean your title.

MACHIAVELLI: Yes. I would ask you not to compare *The Prince* with the book it seems to contradict the most, the book that is the most famous and influential one in all of philosophy, at least up until my time—

SOCRATES: Plato's *Republic*, you mean?

MACHIAVELLI: Yes. I know he was your favorite pupil, but—

SOCRATES: You do *not* know that. Actually, I have many problems with that book. You may be interested to know that it will continue to be the most influential book in the history of philosophy for many centuries, and that is why it is natural to compare it with your book. For they were the two pioneers of classical and modern political philosophy as well as a classic contrast of temperaments: what a man named William James will call the tender-minded versus the tough-minded, the idealist versus the realist, the rationalist versus the empiricist, principles versus facts

—it seems a perfect setup. Why do you ask me not to use this comparison?

MACHIAVELLI: The answer is in the two titles. I wrote my book for a single reader: the man who is or wants to be a prince. I told him simply what works and what does not work—for him, for the prince. Plato wrote his *Republic* for a whole society, a *res publica*, a public reality. The "common good" always takes precedence over the private good in *The Republic*.

SOCRATES: This is a fact.

MACHIAVELLI: And a second difference is that Plato's *res publica*, or public reality, was *not* a reality but a dream. When Plato himself tried to make his dream real in Syracuse, at the invitation of its ruler, his cousin Dion, it did not work at all. It was a disaster. *The Republic* is written to a man who does not exist: ideal human nature in the abstract.

SOCRATES: The disaster in Syracuse is also a fact. But whether or not ideal human nature exists is one of the great philosophical questions on which you differed with Plato. He was a metaphysical realist; he thought the *nature* of a thing was as real as the thing. But you were a nominalist: you thought that natures were only *nomina*, words, and that only concrete individual things were real. But your book is not about metaphysics, so we shall not argue that issue today—though it is useful to remember that many of your arguments in *The Prince* presuppose your metaphysical premise of nominalism. It is the other assumption, about the common good and the private good, that most sharply distinguishes your book, and your title, from Plato's. It seems right to argue about that here. Why do you ask me not to do so?

MACHIAVELLI: Because our purposes were wholly different. Plato claimed to define ideal social justice; I did not. I claimed to define the means to the end of political success; he did not.

SOCRATES: Fair enough, Niccolò. I accept that clarification. I shall confine my questioning to the pages of *your* book.

MACHIAVELLI: Thank you, Socrates. You are more fair than I had thought you would be.

SOCRATES: What do you mean by "fair"? Is it the same as "just"? If so, why can we not discuss Plato's question and try to define justice?

MACHIAVELLI: I retract my compliment.

SOCRATES: I retract my question. I was teasing you, Niccolò. I shall confine my questioning to the pages of *your* book.

MACHIAVELLI: Thank you.

SOCRATES: You begin, in chapter 1, by classifying all states into republics and principalities. Why do you begin there?

MACHIAVELLI: Because you must know first the general layout, and then later the details, of whatever you want to master. I am writing to a prince, real or erstwhile—

SOCRATES: People no longer say "erstwhile", except in Oxford and Cambridge. They say "wannabe".

MACHIAVELLI: If all your corrections are that mild, I'm in for an easy Purgatory, I think.

SOCRATES: Alas, no. For now comes the *least* mild of all the questions that need to be asked.

MACHIAVELLI: Do what you must, Socrates.

3

The First Principle
of *The Prince*

SOCRATES: My first question is about your first principle.

MACHIAVELLI: Why am I not surprised about that?

SOCRATES: Why are you sarcastic at my logic?

MACHIAVELLI: I am suspicious of your method. You rationalistic philosophers love to begin with "first principles". But I prefer to begin with the facts and derive my principles from the facts and justify them by the facts, as scientists test their hypotheses by their data.

SOCRATES: Oh, I do, too. I shall be doing just that: testing your hypotheses by data as well as by logic. I don't see why you oppose those two methods: they complement each other.

MACHIAVELLI: I do not oppose them.

SOCRATES: Then you should not object to my examining your principles as well as your data.

MACHIAVELLI: Examine away, then. What do you take to be my first principle?

SOCRATES: It is the one mentioned at the end of your first little chapter. You say that a prince wins a dominion in one of two ways: either by *virtù* or by *fortuna*.

MACHIAVELLI: Or by a combination of both.

SOCRATES: So you classify all that happens in human history as due to these two forces, correct?

MACHIAVELLI: Yes.

SOCRATES: So this is your first, most basic principle of explanation, is it not?

MACHIAVELLI: Yes. But I did not *begin* with this principle and then try to deduce anything from it. I derived it from my study of the facts of history. It is a scientific principle, not a philosophical one. I believe I was the first person to make history a science.

SOCRATES: How did you do that? What did you do that no one before you had done?

MACHIAVELLI: I discovered its most basic categories. You see, *virtù* and *fortuna* are in the science of history what *matter*, *space*, and *time* are in the science of cosmology.

SOCRATES: ("Physics" is the name they will give that science in later times.) I see. Like the basic categories of *mind*, *emotions*, and *will* in the science of psychology. And how do you understand the importance of such basic categories? Why do you claim that your discovery of the basic categories of human history make you the first to make history a science?

MACHIAVELLI: Basic categories empower us through knowledge.

SOCRATES: So the end of categories is knowledge, and the end of knowledge is power?

MACHIAVELLI: Exactly. When we know the basic categories in any field, we are able to summarize a vast variety of phenomena under a single formula; and this, in turn, enables us to predict and thus control these phenomena. And that is what makes for a practical science.

SOCRATES: Excellently said, Niccolò. You are a very intelligent man, and your understanding of the nature of a practical science was far ahead of most thinkers of your time.

MACHIAVELLI: Thank you, Socrates. But I am still fearful of what you called "the least mild of all the questions that need to be asked". Was that the question you already asked me, and have I satisfied you with my answer?

SOCRATES: No, the "least mild question" is still to come. But first tell me what you mean by your basic categories and, then, how you use them in your basic formula for your science of history, or politics, or whatever we are to call it.

MACHIAVELLI: It's very simple, Socrates. *Virtù* means prowess, ability, potency, power: all the powers by which a man may control history by controlling the lives and behavior of other men, whether by arms or by laws or by persuasion. And *fortuna* means all the forces that control human life that we ourselves cannot, in turn, control. In other words, chance or luck, whether good or bad.

SOCRATES: I see. So *virtù* does not mean "moral virtue" and *fortuna* does not mean a "fortune" in money. *Virtù* means power and being able to exercise power and control, while *fortuna* means its opposite, being on the receiving end. Is that right?

MACHIAVELLI: You understand my terms correctly, Socrates.

SOCRATES: And all that is not under our control you call chance or luck?

MACHIAVELLI: Yes.

SOCRATES: That may be an assumption we will have to question at some time. But for now, I want to know how you use these categories to make your truth claim, your proposition. What do you say with these terms, Niccolò? What is your basic formula?

MACHIAVELLI: It is the basic formula for success in any field, Socrates, but especially in the affairs of state, and most especially for one who is a prince—a ruler —if he aspires to be a successful one, and even a great one. It is also for one who is not a prince but who aspires to be one.

And it is this: success is the maximization of *virtù* and the minimization of *fortuna*. Failure is the opposite.

SOCRATES: Admirably clear and simple, Niccolò!

MACHIAVELLI: Thank you. By the way, I would appreciate it if you would address me by my title and my family name, as is proper, rather than calling me "Niccolò", as though we were children at play.

SOCRATES: Everyone is known by his familiar name here. There are no titles, not even for emperors. For we *are* all only children at play—as you will eventually understand. But these deeper matters will be taken care of later. I am only your first preliminary therapist here; I deal only with your book.

So let us return to it and its most fundamental formula.

MACHIAVELLI: Which you called "admirably clear and simple".

SOCRATES: I did.

MACHIAVELLI: So what is this "least mild question" you threaten me with?

SOCRATES: No one threatens here, Niccolò. Oh, stop looking so shocked; surely you must have suspected that. Did you really think the advice in your book would work as well here as it did down there in the cave of shadows?

MACHIAVELLI: So that is why you refused me when I made you an offer you couldn't refuse.

SOCRATES: Of course. But we must now ask the question I called "the least mild" and you called "threatening". It is a question about your book's fundamental thesis, your formula for success.

MACHIAVELLI: Let it come, then, no matter how clever or complex. I am not afraid. What about my thesis? It is "admirably clear and simple", you say. What more do you want?

SOCRATES: Oh, just a little simple thing: we must inquire whether it is true.

MACHIAVELLI: True?

SOCRATES: Is there an echo in here?

MACHIAVELLI: True? True? That's all?

SOCRATES: A double echo, I believe.

MACHIAVELLI: But—what is truth?

SOCRATES: I would very strongly advise you not to play that gambit. The one who made that question famous has suffered a severe setback to his reputation for all time—something I think you want to avoid, no?

MACHIAVELLI: Yes, yes, of course.

SOCRATES: Well, then, there are two ways of proving any proposition true, as I know you know from your study of logic: deductively and inductively. The first is by far the quicker way, if it can be done—which is one reason why I tended to prefer it in my dialogues. My dialogue partner always seemed to be in a hurry to do something else than to seek and find the truth.

MACHIAVELLI: Then let us try the quick road first. If it can get us to our destination, we would waste much time taking longer roads. I believe my thesis is what logicians call self-evidently true and, thus, irrefutable. For all that happens is either under our control or not; thus all falls into either *virtù* or *fortuna*. There can be no quarrel with the categories and no third category. That is what we should call my preliminary thesis: that all comes about either by *virtù* or by *fortuna*. And my main thesis is my formula for success: that success is the maximization of *virtù* and the minimization of *fortuna*. That, too, is self-evident, for *virtù* means "control", and that is what we mean by "success".

I hope you will be pleased, Socrates, that I have condescended to use the kind of argument you philosophers prefer: an abstract and deductive rather than a concrete and inductive one, to save much time, so that you need not investigate all the other arguments in my book and all the historical details on which I based my conclusion.

If I have passed your inquest, what is my next step? Where do you send me now?

SOCRATES: How hasty you newly arrived mortals are! We have hardly begun, and yet already you speak of the next step, as if we had finished.

MACHIAVELLI: But I thought I had just satisfied you and your single-minded love of truth. I logically proved both of my two theses to be necessarily true. You cannot contradict either without committing a logical self-contradiction. Surely that is your supreme standard of truth?

SOCRATES: Niccolò, suppose I announced to you these two great and world-changing teachings: first, that all goats are either white or not white; and second, that the formula for whiteness in goats is this: since we mean the same thing by "white" as we mean by "colorless", a goat is white to the extent that it is colorless. Both these theses are logically self-evident, are they not? They are necessarily true. But they tell me nothing. I am no wiser after I understand them than I was before. It is like telling me that narwhals are narwhals instead of telling me that narwhals are swimming mammals with a single horn. Both halves of your great formula are what logicians call mere tautologies. They are true but trivial.

MACHIAVELLI: But this is exactly what you philosophers fill your books with and what I do not. My book is full of facts, not windy words.

SOCRATES: That remains to be seen.

MACHIAVELLI: So let us see it. You said you would examine my *book*, not just my principles. To do that, we must open the pages, and open our eyes and explore this storehouse of facts.

SOCRATES: We must, indeed. But shall we do it for the sake of knowing only these facts themselves or for the sake of knowing the new science of history that you claim to have found? For a science must contain not only facts but also principles and formulas, must it not? If these come at the beginning, we deduce more particular conclusions from them. If they come at the end of an induction that begins with many particular facts, we arrive at these general principles as our conclusions. In either case, we need general principles. How can there be any kind of science without principles? Or do you claim to have invented a new kind of science?

MACHIAVELLI: No, Socrates. You are right: we must combine facts and principles. My wisdom is not in the mere knowledge of facts or in principles that do not touch and wrestle with facts, principles that are mere tautologies; but it is in deriving the practical principles of political science from the facts of history.

SOCRATES: So it is the principles that are your chief claim to wisdom.

MACHIAVELLI: Yes—but not just the principles themselves but how they are solidly derived from the facts of past history and, above all, how they are useful for a prince to apply to change future history.

SOCRATES: And these principles must not be mere tautologies? They must teach us something we do not know already?

MACHIAVELLI: Yes.

SOCRATES: Then I think I have found one such principle, at least, in your book about which we can argue—is it true or not?—once we have exposed it and formulated it. So it seems to me that this should be our next quest. Does this seem proper to you?

MACHIAVELLI: I suspend my judgment on your method of procedure until I see its results.

SOCRATES: How very suspicious of you! Will you at least come with me on this quest through the landscape of your own book?

MACHIAVELLI: I think you have made me an offer I can't refuse, Socrates. So let's proceed.

4

The Test of Truth

SOCRATES: We are searching for some general principle that is not a mere tautology, one that the mass of mankind does not already know and that requires a wise teacher like yourself to discover it.

MACHIAVELLI: And it will be a *practical* principle, unlike those of your philosophy, or at least those of your disciple Plato. For my book, unlike *The Republic*, is a practical book.

SOCRATES: And what is the test of a practical principle, in your mind? What makes a principle practical?

MACHIAVELLI: If we know and use it, it will turn failure into success, defeat into victory, impotence into power; and if we do not know it, or know it but do not use it, it explains why we fail.

SOCRATES: Will a practical principle do this if it is false?

MACHIAVELLI: No. Only if it is true.

SOCRATES: This is your test of truth for it, then?

MACHIAVELLI: Yes.

SOCRATES: And therefore also your test of falsehood if it is false: that the man who acts on it would fail if it is false, just as he would succeed if it is true.

MACHIAVELLI: I suppose so. Why do you insist on adding the test of falsehood as well as truth?

SOCRATES: Because we require a principle that is not a bare tautology, do we not?

MACHIAVELLI: Yes—

SOCRATES: And therefore one that tells us something that some do not know?

MACHIAVELLI: Yes.

SOCRATES: And those who do not know it is true might think it false?

MACHIAVELLI: Yes.

SOCRATES: And if the principle is indeed true, then those who think it false, and who act according to their false thought, will *not* succeed but will fail, at least more often than those who believe and apply the principle?

MACHIAVELLI: Yes. That must follow.

SOCRATES: And we can observe this failure in the world of facts, the world of visible appearances?

MACHIAVELLI: Precisely.

SOCRATES: So your principle will be both verifiable in experience, if it is true, and falsifiable in experience, if it is false.

MACHIAVELLI: Yes, Socrates. That is what a practical scientific principle must be.

SOCRATES: Good. Now I have a second question about the principle we are looking for. What will this principle be *about*? What real thing will it reveal in a new and true way?

MACHIAVELLI: I don't understand what you are asking.

SOCRATES: Let me tell you the *kind* of principle I think it must be by giving you another such principle, one that I believe to be true but that I think you do not, but one that is *about* the same thing that your principle must be about. Do you understand?

MACHIAVELLI: Yes.

SOCRATES: My principle is that no man knowingly does evil, that all evil is ignorance.

MACHIAVELLI: A totally ridiculous principle if there ever was one!

SOCRATES: Perhaps, but I do not want to argue about its truth or falsity, but only to show you what *kind* of principle I think we must look for: one that makes a difference and teaches us something new, not about the nature of numbers or the stars or books or the gods, but about the nature of man. I think that is what you want in a practical principle, isn't it?

MACHIAVELLI: I agree. That is exactly what I claim to know: the nature of man. Unlike you, poor Socrates! Your eyes were fixed on the stars and not on the earth. You confused man with a god or an angel. If there is any topic you need my wisdom about, that is it. If there is any topic I shall pass your test on, this is it.

SOCRATES: Because my idea of the nature of man was simplistic and one-sided, while yours is fuller and more complex?

MACHIAVELLI: Yes. And because mine therefore works. Mine comes from the facts and is tested by the facts, not abstract theories.

SOCRATES: We shall see about these two claims: that your philosophy of man is realistic in being true to the whole complexity of human nature and behavior, and that it is realistic in being true to observable facts. For that is your main claim to fame, is it not?—that you are the realist?

MACHIAVELLI: Indeed! Especially as compared with you, the famous idealist. I am confident that I can show you that you need my wisdom and my assistance.

SOCRATES: I hope you can show me your wisdom. Back in the other world, I never did succeed in my lifelong quest to find a wise man. I concluded that only God is wise and that man is only wisdom's lover and that the first and best wisdom any man could have on earth was *that* wisdom, the wisdom of knowing his own unwisdom. I hope you can show me that my conclusion was premature and that there was a man of wisdom in the world, if only I had had the opportunity to meet him.

MACHIAVELLI: My wisdom may not be the kind *you* are looking for, Socrates.

SOCRATES: Oh, I will grant you your very different purpose. My only question will be whether you fulfilled your purpose, not whether you fulfilled mine. I will not judge you by the standards of my philosophy but by those of your own.

MACHIAVELLI: I am very pleased at that. I see there is justice in Purgatory. Thank you, Socrates.

SOCRATES: But as for your other hope, that you can show me how I need your assistance here and should employ you—I have no authority to do so. I am under higher authorities.

MACHIAVELLI: Yes, yes, of course. But I know how authority works, I assure you.

SOCRATES: I wonder whether you do.

MACHIAVELLI: What do you think is my error?

SOCRATES: You misplace the word "the".

MACHIAVELLI: What?

SOCRATES: You confuse God the Father with the Godfather. In your world, you learned to make someone an offer he couldn't refuse. In this world, we work by a different method. *His* method, you see, is to make you an offer you *can* refuse. His authority respects your freedom.

MACHIAVELLI: It is strange to call that kind of wimpy attitude "authority".

SOCRATES: I *thought* you misunderstood authority. You wrote in your book that "it is better to be feared than to be loved." He does not share your preference. He would rather be loved than feared.

MACHIAVELLI: I do not understand that. But since I am in his world now, and not mine, I must accept it,

I suppose. Far be it from me to fail to show respect for whatever my superiors demand!

SOCRATES: But I fear you will find that more than *respect* is demanded.

MACHIAVELLI: Whatever it takes. What else is demanded?

SOCRATES: Truth. He is an absolute stickler for truth.

MACHIAVELLI: Oh, so am I. That is why I wrote my book: to tell the truth; to show how many things are in fact, not in the ideal.

SOCRATES: Then let us examine your book.

MACHIAVELLI: Sentence by sentence?

SOCRATES: No, I will not be "picky" but will confine myself to your most important principles and formulas.

MACHIAVELLI: The *political* formulas.

SOCRATES: The philosophical *foundations* of your practical political formulas.

MACHIAVELLI: You mean my understanding of human nature, my psychology or anthropology.

SOCRATES: Yes, that to begin with. Second, how it yields an ethic. And third, how both necessarily imply a metaphysic, a general theory of reality, of what is real and what is unreal. And then also, in the fourth place, an epistemology, a theory of knowledge and method, to justify the way you arrived at your knowledge. And finally, your logic: whether you are at least consistent with yourself or whether you contradict your own deepest premises or highest ends.

MACHIAVELLI: I suppose if they send a *philosopher* to examine me, I must expect an examination structured according to the basic divisions of philosophy. I am willing to begin with my philosophy of man. What do you want to examine first?

SOCRATES: Your first principle, of course.

MACHIAVELLI: Examine away, then.

SOCRATES: We have to do something else first.

MACHIAVELLI: How tedious you are! What?

SOCRATES: We have to *find* it before we can examine it.

MACHIAVELLI: Oh. Well, then—let us find it.

SOCRATES: Unfortunately, there is something else that we must do first, before we can find it.

MACHIAVELLI: You are unbelievably tedious, Socrates! You also surprise me. What do you say comes before finding the first principle?

SOCRATES: May I suggest looking for it first?

MACHIAVELLI: Perhaps you are wiser than I thought. Well, let us begin.

SOCRATES: An appropriate thing for beginners to do.

5

Machiavelli's
Philosophy of Man

SOCRATES: I would like to begin with a typical passage of practical advice.

MACHIAVELLI: Good! I trust you understand that practical advice was the whole purpose of my book, not theory or sermons, not metaphysics or morals.

SOCRATES: Of course, I understand that. You said so in your book.

MACHIAVELLI: I thought I said that as clearly as possible. And yet many readers, probably *most* readers, criticized me for writing a book I never wrote. *The Prince* is not a bad moral book because it is not a moral book at all. I make no claims about morality, about man as he ought to be—only about anthropology, about man as he is. And I make no claims about metaphysics, either, about timeless truths; only about history, about the past, the present, and the future, about what can be seen with the eye and inferred by inductive reasoning. Metaphysicians make claims about the unseen, and they argue endlessly. I am not a metaphysician. I am an anthropologist.

SOCRATES: I understand your intention. But I suspect most of your readers do, too, since you stated it so clearly in your book. But those readers may wonder, as I do, whether it is *possible* to do anthropology without doing metaphysics.

MACHIAVELLI: Of course it is possible. I did it!

SOCRATES: Did you? Let us see. What do you mean by anthropology?

MACHIAVELLI: The scientific study of man—of man as he is and has been, not of man as he ought to be.

SOCRATES: Is it possible to know "man as he is" without knowing something about what is? For instance, if "gods" are not included in "what is" but man *is* included in "what is", then man cannot be a god. Is that not a reasonable argument?

MACHIAVELLI: Of course it is.

SOCRATES: But it presupposes a metaphysic, in claiming that "what is" does not include gods. For metaphysics is the study of all that is and is not.

MACHIAVELLI: Oh.

SOCRATES: The only way I know to say nothing about what is, is to say nothing.

MACHIAVELLI: Oh, well, if that's all you mean by metaphysics, let it be so, then. I was doing metaphysics. But at least I was not doing morality.

SOCRATES: But you were. You yourself drew many important moral conclusions from your anthropology, just as you presupposed many important metaphysical premises in your anthropology. For instance, in chapter 18, about whether princes should keep their promises, you justify your answer to this moral question about what princes *should* do (which is the answer "no, not always") by your anthropology: **"[I]f all men were good, this advice would be bad; but since men are wicked and will not keep faith with you, you need not keep faith with them."** Wootton, p. 54, ll. 23–25.

MACHIAVELLI: I know that many readers were shocked at my teaching that, but I can defend it—

SOCRATES: Oh, perhaps you can. I am not questioning that now. Later, we will inquire whether you speak *truly*. Now, we are only inquiring whether you speak philosophically: that is to say, whether your anthropology leads to a morality and whether it is based on a metaphysic, as I claim and you deny.

MACHIAVELLI: Neither! It comes from my observation of visible facts, not from theories or principles; and it leads to factual, practical success in this world, not to ideal saintliness for the next.

SOCRATES: Excuse me, but where do you think we are?

MACHIAVELLI: A slip of the tongue. I do not know where we are, but I hope we are in the place of justice.

SOCRATES: We are.

MACHIAVELLI: Then I trust you will be just enough to judge me by my own claims and promises.

SOCRATES: That is my intention.

MACHIAVELLI: Then you will not impose your deductive method upon my inductive one. I do not hunt for truth in the zoo cages of abstract formulas, but in the jungle of concrete facts. You philosophers turn loose the animals from their cages and tell them to run into the jungle: you begin with the caged animals of principles and then try to apply them to real life. I go into the jungle like a hunter to *find* the principles where they actually live; *then* I cage them in formulas.

SOCRATES: I shall therefore tailor my investigation to your method, not mine. We shall begin with particulars.

MACHIAVELLI: Thank you.

SOCRATES: For instance, in chapter 3 of *The Prince*—

MACHIAVELLI: Finally we talk about my book instead of talking about talking!

SOCRATES: You give advice to a prince concerning the planting of colonies in a territory he has newly conquered—

MACHIAVELLI: Why do you choose *this* passage, Socrates?

SOCRATES: Because I am on a hunting expedition. The beast I seek is the fundamental truth claim of your anthropology, and I think I can best find it in this part of the jungle.

MACHIAVELLI: Fair enough.

SOCRATES: You say:

> **Colonies do not cost much to run. You will have to lay out little or nothing to establish and maintain them. You will only offend those from whom you seize fields and houses to give to your settlers, and they will be only**

a tiny minority within the territory. Those whom you offend will be scattered and become poor, so they will be unable to do you any harm. All the rest will remain uninjured, and so ought to remain quiet; at the same time they will be afraid to make a false move, for they will have before them the fate of their neighbors as an example of what may happen to them. . . . There is a general rule to be noted here: People should either be caressed or crushed. If you do them minor damage they will get their revenge; but if you cripple them there is nothing they can do. If you need to injure someone, do it in such a way that you do not have to fear their vengeance.

Wootton, p. 9, ll. 28–36, 39–40; p. 10, ll. 1–3.

MACHIAVELLI: You will not find any advice more practical than that! History proves it true.

SOCRATES: Since that is your claim, I think I must reverse my method. I usually like to find a principle and formulate it before judging whether it is true or false. But perhaps just for this once it would work better if we reversed that order, strange as that seems, and begin with the question that seems easier to answer in this case—is it true? does history verify it, as you claim?—and then proceed to the harder, subtler question of how exactly to formulate this principle we are in search of. For this formula may be lurking behind your arguments, like a tiger hiding behind a bush, and if we expose your argument, we may expose your principle as a hunter exposes a tiger by exploring in the bush.

MACHIAVELLI: I don't see how this will work, but I am willing to accompany you, O mighty hunter, down your reversed path. What do you want to investigate about my advice that you just quoted?

SOCRATES: Simply whether history verifies it, as you say.

MACHIAVELLI: Fine. But you need a historian for that —someone like me. You are only a philosopher.

SOCRATES: But I have been in this place for an immense time and have met men from many times and places in history, even those you would have called future times when you were alive on earth. Time works differently in this place.

MACHIAVELLI: What do you know of future history, Socrates? Tell me, I beg you.

SOCRATES: I will tell you enough to fulfill our present quest. In the latter half of the twentieth century there was a nation that followed your advice about establishing colonies, or settlements, in lands they had conquered in war from another people. The nation was Israel, which was established in 1948 in lands that were taken from an Arab people called Palestinians. This was the first time the Jews had had a homeland in about eighteen centuries. The Palestinians, with the help of more powerful Arab neighbors, including Egypt, initiated three wars to get back this land. Instead, they lost *more* Arab lands to Israel. After each war the Jews built settlements in the conquered lands and installed their own citizens in them.

MACHIAVELLI: Wise strategy.

SOCRATES: But it did not work. It repeatedly provoked the Palestinians and other Arabs to violence, for decades. They even resorted to suicide missions just to spread terror and death among the Jews. No matter what the Jews did—negotiations, compromise, return of the conquered land, or retaliation, raids, and repression, nothing brought about stability and peace. When the Palestinians had no guns, they threw stones at the armed soldiers of Israel.

MACHIAVELLI: The Jews should have answered the violence with greater violence if they had the military capacity.

SOCRATES: They did.

MACHIAVELLI: What was the result?

SOCRATES: It did not deter the violence.

MACHIAVELLI: The force should have been lethal. Dead men cannot revenge wrongs.

SOCRATES: It *was* lethal.

MACHIAVELLI: What? Did the Arab ghosts rise from the grave? Did the dead take revenge?

SOCRATES: No, but the living did. For they had a connection with the dead. Perhaps this is a fact about human nature that you failed to take into account when you wrote, **"All the rest will remain uninjured, and so ought to remain quiet."**

MACHIAVELLI: What fact do you mean?

SOCRATES: It has various names. "Solidarity" is one. "Community" is another. "Loyalty" is a third. Do you claim these words do not refer to real forces in human nature?

MACHIAVELLI: They are *ideals*. They may have moved some men, at some times, in some circumstances, as beautiful objects of mental contemplation and moral aspiration. But the desire to avoid pain and violent death moves all men at all times, because it moves them, not as ideals that need to be made real, but as already existing drives within their nature.

SOCRATES: So in the terms made famous by my philosophical grandson, Aristotle, moral ideals move men as final causes, not as efficient causes—is that what you say?

MACHIAVELLI: Exactly.

SOCRATES: So in a state of mere nature, or pure nature, where man's behavior is determined only by that which exists by nature, within human nature, each individual would be selfish and competitive?

MACHIAVELLI: Of course.

SOCRATES: So the state of nature is a state of war?

MACHIAVELLI: Exactly. Why do you suppose all men at all times in history have fought wars? It is obviously in their very nature.

SOCRATES: But men have also at all times in history cooperated with each other and formed societies and made laws. Why is this not equally in their nature?

MACHIAVELLI: When a man thinks he can achieve his natural end best by cooperation, he cooperates. When he thinks he can achieve it best by war, he wars.

SOCRATES: But the end he seeks by both is the same?

MACHIAVELLI: Yes. It is the expansion of his own being, his possessions, his power, and his control by conquest.

SOCRATES: The triumph of *virtù* over *fortuna*.

MACHIAVELLI: Exactly. No man wants to be controlled; all want to control. No one wants to be weak, enslaved, ignorant, or—above all—tortured or killed. *That* is natural.

SOCRATES: How, then, does morality come about?

MACHIAVELLI: Men discover that this end can often be more effectively attained by cooperating and making laws. These laws they then declare to be "real" and "natural". And these laws define morality for them. So they come to speak of moral ideals as if they were parts of the real natural universe, like the stars, as if they were parts of *fortuna* in their lives, things discovered rather than invented; and also as preexisting attributes of their nature, like their bones, rather than as things like clothes that they invented to shelter and cover their poor nature.

SOCRATES: You know, you sound very much like a philosopher who would come shortly after you and expand your sketchy philosophy into a complete system: Thomas Hobbes. Also like a man with whom I once argued about justice: Thrasymachos.

MACHIAVELLI: I have read Plato's account of that conversation in the *Republic*. By the way, did you really invent all those wacky ideas, or was it Plato?

SOCRATES: Oh, nearly everything in the *Republic* is Plato's, except for book 1, where I conversed with

Thrasymachos. I never ventured into politics, as Plato did, for the god forbade me, as I explained in my *Apology*. But let us not be distracted: an idea's inventor is not important; its truth is. And we must now inquire whether your idea, that justice and morality and co-operation and unselfishness are not natural to man, is true or false.

MACHIAVELLI: You argued against Thrasymachos by mere logic. But I argue on the basis of facts and observation of how men actually do behave. So how can we argue this issue on common grounds? We use opposite methods, you and I. Your idealistic, rationalistic method naturally yields your idealistic, rationalistic conclusions. My realistic, empirical method yields my realistic conclusions. A book like Plato's *Republic*, whose aim is to define the concept of ideal justice, may use a method like yours. But a book like *The Prince*, whose aim is practical rather than theoretical, must use a more scientific, empirical method. It is unfair for you to judge me by your methods. Again I appeal to your own ideal of fairness, of justice. Will you practice what you preach or not?

SOCRATES: I will.

MACHIAVELLI: Then practice justice, and evaluate me justly.

SOCRATES: That is precisely my intention.

MACHIAVELLI: Good. Then let us look at facts rather than theories.

SOCRATES: Let us, indeed. Let us test your theories, your claims, by facts. Especially your theory that there is no moral force innate to man; that justice is an invention rather than a discovery; that morality is artificial rather than natural; that what some call "conscience" and others call "moral authority" is *not* a deep, powerful, and ineradicable part of human nature, as most men and most cultures have believed.

MACHIAVELLI: The fact that proves this theory of mine is the fact that other cultures invent other laws. Surely you are not ignorant of the facts of history, Socrates? Are you still so provincial that you think the whole world thinks in Greek?

SOCRATES: No, indeed. For instance, I know of the Chinese, whose language contains a word—*Tao*—remarkably similar in its range of meanings to the Greek words *dike* and *logos*. *Tao* means "the way of nature", "the way of wisdom in human affairs", and "the way of ultimate reality" all in one. *Logos* means "reason", "meaning", and "order", and then "word" or "speech" revealing this order. *Dike* also means "order" but especially "justice", or "moral order". Both cultures reveal in their language that they see moral goodness as real, more real than the stars and just as natural.

MACHIAVELLI: Then both cultures err. Men are fools. Surely you know that, Socrates.

SOCRATES: Is *that* the fundamental principle of your anthropology?

MACHIAVELLI: Not quite.

SOCRATES: There is also another Chinese word, *te*, which expresses just the opposite view of man's nature from yours. And it is the view of nearly all cultures and traditions. The word means a person's inherent "moral force" or "moral authority". It is to conscience what color is to sight, sound to hearing, or quantity to calculation.

MACHIAVELLI: I don't understand.

SOCRATES: I know you don't. I appreciate your honesty. I shall try to show you what I mean. Take this passage from *The Prince*—

MACHIAVELLI: It's about time we returned to our data!

SOCRATES: In chapter 14, **"What a Ruler Should Do As Regards the Militia"**, you write: **"There is simply no comparison between a man who is unarmed and one who is not. It is unreasonable to expect that an armed man should obey one who is unarmed."**

Bull, p. 88, ll. 7–10.

MACHIAVELLI: I—

SOCRATES: Please let me quote one more passage before we argue or explain. Data, Niccolò, we need data first, remember? In chapter 6 you write, **"Let us look at those who through their own skill [*virtù*], and not merely through chance [*fortuna*], have become rulers. In my view, the greatest have been Moses, Cyrus, Romulus, Theseus and others like them."** And later in that chapter you announce this general principle: **"[A]ll armed prophets have succeeded and all unarmed ones have failed."** And you support this principle with your examples, your data: **"Moses, Cyrus, Theseus, and Romulus would not**

Wootton, p. 18, ll. 35–38.

Donno, p. 27, ll. 24–25.

have been able to make their peoples obey their new structures of authority for long if they had been unarmed. This is what happened, in our own day, to Friar Girolamo Savonarola. He and his new constitution were destroyed as soon as the multitude began to stop believing in him." Wootton, p. 20, ll. 20–25.

MACHIAVELLI: Good; now we are on solid ground: historical facts. Do you know how the same citizens who loved and obeyed that preacher and moralist Savonarola soon turned against him when he continued to denounce their cherished luxuries and vices and burned him at the stake?

SOCRATES: Yes. And I know you were there and saw it all—that is, you saw what was visible. I wonder, however, whether you see what is invisible.

MACHIAVELLI: This *te*, or "moral force", you mean?

SOCRATES: Yes. As we noted, you write, **"There is simply no comparison between a man who is unarmed and one who is not."** But this is true only of their arms. **"There is no comparison"** because arms are present in the one but absent in the other. But there *is* a comparison in the men themselves. For after all, an *armed* man is an armed *man* and an *unarmed* man is an unarmed *man*, so there *is* a comparison after all between the two men: in whatever pertains to man as man.

MACHIAVELLI: And you include this *te*, or moral force, under that category?

SOCRATES: Yes. Unlike arms, it is not visible. But surely it is a human thing.

MACHIAVELLI: A pleasing theory, but I have not observed this "human thing" as a fact.

SOCRATES: Let us see. You observed Savonarola's failure, did you not?

MACHIAVELLI: Yes.

SOCRATES: Did you also observe his earlier success?

MACHIAVELLI: Yes.

SOCRATES: Did you observe its cause?

MACHIAVELLI: Its cause? What do you mean?

SOCRATES: Things have causes, do they not? Is this not a basic principle of all science? How else do we account for things, if not by their causes?

MACHIAVELLI: True.

SOCRATES: So how do you account for Savonarola's earlier success as an unarmed prophet, if not by *te*?

MACHIAVELLI: I am not denying that some men are moved by moral conviction. I am just denying that this force is strong or lasting or deeply rooted in human nature, as is the fear of pain and the force of arms.

SOCRATES: How, then, do you account for Moses' success? No prophet in history has had his laws take hold of more people for more time. The Mosaic moral law has structured Western civilization for almost four thousand years. Where were Moses' arms? You list him along with Cyrus, Theseus, and Romulus, who murdered his brother Remus, then founded Rome.

MACHIAVELLI: And if Remus had had the arms and Romulus had lacked them, the most successful empire in history would have been called the Reman instead of the Roman!

SOCRATES: Perhaps. But where were *Moses'* arms? Did the Bible forget to count his horses and chariots, perhaps? Did his navy ferry his people across the Red Sea?

MACHIAVELLI: Even if I cannot explain Moses, I explain the other three. Three wins, one loss is a good percentage.

SOCRATES: Not for a scientist. A universal formula must apply to all cases, not just some. Here is an unarmed prophet who did not fail, as you say he must.

MACHIAVELLI: I answered that objection in my book.

SOCRATES: Where you wrote, **"Obviously, we should not discuss Moses' skill, for he was a mere agent, following the instructions given him by God"**? Wootton, p. 19, ll. 1–2.

MACHIAVELLI: Yes.

SOCRATES: But this is not what a scientist says: "We should not discuss these empirical facts, since they conflict with my theory"!

MACHIAVELLI: Moses is an isolated anomaly. The exception proves the rule.

SOCRATES: What a silly saying that is! An exception *disproves* a rule. One black swan disproves the rule that all swans are white.

MACHIAVELLI: Let it be an isolated error, then. I never claimed to be infallible. One man, Moses, I cannot explain. All other men I can. So my formula still is very useful.

SOCRATES: Only if we forget the most powerful man in history.

MACHIAVELLI: Whom do you mean?

SOCRATES: Would you not define power as that which causes changes or makes differences, and the greatest power as that which causes the greatest changes or makes the greatest difference to the most lives?

MACHIAVELLI: Yes. That is a good definition of power.

SOCRATES: Then tell me, who has ever made a greater difference to more lives than Jesus?

MACHIAVELLI: No one.

SOCRATES: So tell me, where were his arms?

MACHIAVELLI: I do not claim to explain the supernatural.

SOCRATES: And do you call *te*, or moral force, supernatural?

MACHIAVELLI: No.

SOCRATES: Then it must be natural. But you denied that, too.

MACHIAVELLI: It is neither a natural nor a supernatural reality because it is not a reality at all. It is an idea or an ideal.

SOCRATES: We must explore your notion of the relation between the real and the ideal later, when we explore your metaphysics. But for now, you seem to be backing away when the facts seem to refute your theory rather than using your theory to explain the

facts. Is this how a scientist thinks? Is this not precisely the charge you lay against the philosophers?
Which of the two of us is now open to all the data?

MACHIAVELLI: *I* am, because I admit man's evil as
well as man's good. You ignored man's evil, in your
idealism, more than I ignored his good, in my realism.

SOCRATES: But I at least tried to explain the difficult
data—how man can be so evil—by my theory of how
man is by nature good. You do not even try to explain your difficult data—how man can be so good
—by your theory of how man is by nature evil. So
it seems that I, the philosopher and the idealist, am
being scientific in relating my theory to all the data,
while you, the practical, so-called realist, are not.

MACHIAVELLI: Socrates, my unexplained data is only
two men: Moses and Jesus. (The Muslims would
probably challenge me with their prophet Muhammad, too; but I think I can show that his success,
and that of his disciples, was clearly due to force of
arms.) What are two men unexplained compared with
all others explained? Besides, both were Jews, who
were history's most exceptional people. Jesus already
had the advantage of being born into Moses' people,
formed by Moses' morality.

SOCRATES: Then let us look at an example from another culture, to test whether your theory of man
explains the facts. Tell me, please: How would you
explain this happening? A Buddhist monk had a reputation for great wisdom. The greatest Samurai warrior in the territory visited him to hear his wisdom.
But the monk said nothing. "You are a fake!" shouted

the Samurai, drawing his sword. "I will send you to the next world by taking off your head unless you show me one thing that you know and I do not!" "I will show you two", said the monk. "I will show you the gates of Heaven and of Hell." "Now I know you are a fake!" said the warrior. "No," replied the monk, "it is you who are the bigger fake, and also the stupidest and the ugliest man in all the land." At this, the warrior was enraged and drew his sword back to cut off the monk's head. The monk held up one finger and said, "See? I have shown you the gates of Hell." The warrior, impressed with this wisdom and ashamed, sheathed his sword. The monk held up two fingers and said, "And now I have shown you the gate of Heaven."

Tell me, Niccolò, who won this encounter? The armed man or the unarmed man?

MACHIAVELLI: The unarmed man.

SOCRATES: By what force? Do you not here see *te* in action?

MACHIAVELLI: Perhaps so, in this case. But no *state* has ever been governed by such a force. In these few individuals it may be strong, but in most men it is weak. And in politics a prince must take account of the average man and of the masses. That was the subject of my book. Though I wrote it for the individual, the would-be prince, its instruction is not about dealing with individuals, especially unusual and saintly individuals, but about dealing with masses, with states. It is a book of politics, after all.

6

The Existence of *Te*
(Moral Authority)

SOCRATES: Then let us see what you say about *te* in politics—specifically, about states ruled by the *te*, or moral authority, of the Church, "ecclesiastical principalities". In chapter 11 you say:

All that remains for us to discuss, at this point, is the ecclesiastical states. As far as they are concerned, all the problems are encountered before one gets possession of them. One acquires them either through strength [*virtù*] or through luck [*fortuna*], but one can hold on to them without either. For they are maintained by their long-established institutions that are rooted in religion. These have developed to such a pitch of strength they can support their own rulers in power no matter how they live and behave. Only ecclesiastical rulers have states, but no need to defend them; subjects, but no need to govern them. Their states, though they do not defend them, are not taken from them; their subjects, though they do not govern them, do not resent them, and they neither think

Wootton, p.
35, ll. 38–40;
p. 36, ll. 1–10.

of replacing their rulers nor are they in a position to do so. So these are the only rulers who are secure and happy.

A remarkable admission for you to make.

MACHIAVELLI: A simple historical fact. Not an "admission" at all.

SOCRATES: But how can your theory explain that fact?

MACHIAVELLI: What fact?

SOCRATES: The fact of a religious society, of a public social order based on the Christian religion and persisting in it, without compulsion, for more than a thousand years.

MACHIAVELLI: Because men are stupid and sheepish. That is no threat to my anthropology. That is *part* of my anthropology.

SOCRATES: But men are also evil and selfish, you say. Even if the Christian religion is stupid and based on a myth, it demands that man be good and unselfish. Why would men love, and keep, rulers who by their teachings demand that men live contrary to their nature?

MACHIAVELLI: I don't know what goes on in their silly heads, Socrates.

SOCRATES: That is not the answer you gave in your book. You wrote, **"But because they are ruled by a higher power, which human intelligence cannot grasp, I will say no more about them; for, since they have been built up and maintained by God,** Wootton, p.
36, ll. 10–14. **only a presumptuous and rash person would debate about them."**

MACHIAVELLI: There—if you want piety, there it is.

SOCRATES: I never said I wanted piety, only honesty. I am not an Inquisitor, I am a philosopher. And the most flattering description of this passage that I can imagine is "desperate bluffing", as a card player might attempt to bluff when he is on the brink of losing everything. A much less flattering description is also possible: the word that springs to mind is "hypocrisy".

MACHIAVELLI: Why can't you take my words seriously, Socrates?

SOCRATES: Well, let me try to do that, and let us see what results. Tell me, Niccolò, were the vast majority of people in your civilization Catholic?

MACHIAVELLI: Yes. And in the East, Orthodox.

SOCRATES: And if you were to ask any number of them—say, a hundred chosen at random, "What power upholds Christendom?" would all reply that "no one knows", or would they have an answer?

MACHIAVELLI: They would *think* they had an answer.

SOCRATES: And would not all give pretty much the same answer? Would it not be "divine providence" or "divine grace"?

MACHIAVELLI: Yes.

SOCRATES: And do they have any understanding at all of what these terms mean?

MACHIAVELLI: Very little understanding, I think.

SOCRATES: But some?

MACHIAVELLI: Yes.

SOCRATES: Is it the human mind that has this understanding, little though it may be? These ordinary Christians have ordinary human minds, do they not?

MACHIAVELLI: Yes.

SOCRATES: Then, whoever wrote that the ecclesiastical jurisdictions we speak of **"are ruled by a higher power, which human intelligence cannot grasp"** must have been in error. Now who was it who wrote that? I am old and forgetful; please remind me.

Wootton, p. 36, l. 11.

MACHIAVELLI: *I* wrote that, Socrates. But just because they *claim* to know what power it is that upholds the Church's jurisdictions, it does not follow that they *do* know. Surely the distinction I am now making—between knowledge and opinion, or belief —is one on which you have always insisted.

SOCRATES: Yes, it is. So let us consider the alternative: that they do *not* know, but only *believe* they know, the power that upholds these ecclesiastical jurisdictions. For there are only two possibilities. They *believe* they know what force it is that upholds them. Either their belief is true, or it is not. If it is true, then divine grace does uphold them. If their belief is false, then it is not divine grace but some other force.

MACHIAVELLI: Of course. But if they can't *prove* their belief, you would not call it "knowledge" but only "belief", or "right opinion". That's the distinction you keep insisting on yourself, Socrates.

SOCRATES: And I do not forget it here. But the most important distinction here is not between knowledge and right opinion but between right opinion and wrong opinion, true opinion and false opinion.

MACHIAVELLI: Why is that the most important here?

SOCRATES: Because we are examining your book and trying to find your teaching, especially the fundamental principles of your anthropology, your philosophy of man, remember? And our quarry may be hidden in the bushes of your assumptions rather than running through the sunny fields of explicit assertion. So I am trying to coax it out of hiding by some questions.

MACHIAVELLI: Question away, Socrates.

SOCRATES: Please tell me, then, what is the teaching of the Church about this question—the question of what force it is that sustains her? The Church has always been a visible public institution, has she not? Whether she owned much political authority, land, and states, as she did in your day, or none, as in the early days of the martyrs, when she was illegal and persecuted by the Roman emperors, she has always been a public, social, and visible power, ruled by bishops who claim to be the appointed successors to Jesus' apostles—is this not so?

MACHIAVELLI: This is a historical fact, yes.

SOCRATES: So would you tell me, then, what is the Church's answer to the question of what force sustains her public authority, her visible power, however great or small it is? Does she claim that she is sustained by divine grace? Or by some other power, such as ignorance or fear or force of arms?

MACHIAVELLI: *She* maintains it is divine grace; that is why the masses believe it: they certainly did not reason it out for themselves.

SOCRATES: And do you maintain that the Church lies when she says she is upheld by grace?

MACHIAVELLI: No, no, I am not a heretic. I simply said I did not know.

SOCRATES: You said that *no* one knows.

MACHIAVELLI: That is what I said.

SOCRATES: But the Church claims that she knows. And all these Christians claim that they know, too, even though they do not usually claim to be able to prove it.

MACHIAVELLI: Yes, they *claim* that.

SOCRATES: So you disagree with them. You say that no one knows and, therefore, that they do not know and that the Church also does not know what she claims to know.

MACHIAVELLI: You have logically proved that, it seems. What is your next question?

SOCRATES: What is the definition of a heretic?

MACHIAVELLI: So you *are* an Inquisitor in disguise! I *knew* it. How clever these imposters are! And I fell for it, too. Socrates, indeed!

SOCRATES: I assure you I am *not* an Inquisitor. Or an imposter.

MACHIAVELLI: Do you expect me simply to take your word for that? If I assure you I do *not* have a dagger up my sleeve, will you just believe me and take my word for it? How naïve do you think I am, anyway?

SOCRATES: I think you are so naïve that you believe that what you do not see cannot exist. The unseen force of divine grace and the invisible force of the *te*, or moral authority, of men like Moses, Jesus, the Buddhist monk, and even Fra Savonarola for a little while—you do not *see* this, and so you do not believe it exists. I think you are like a tiny child playing peek-a-boo, or like the ostrich hiding its head in the sand, practicing the philosophy of "If I don't see it, it can't be there." Is this not utterly naïve? How could truly practical advice come from one who is so naïve?

7

The Knowledge of
Good and Evil

MACHIAVELLI: Socrates—or whoever you are—you amaze me: you claim I am naïve because I claim that men are wicked, and you claim that you are not naïve because you claim that men are good! This is to turn common sense upside down.

SOCRATES: I do not say that men are only good, but you say that men are only wicked. I take account of evil, but you do not take account of good. That is why I say you are naïve and simplistic and untrue to the complexity of the facts. You claim to be a bold new discoverer of new worlds of truth; but is there a single discovery about human behavior anywhere in your writings that I and most other thinkers in my ancient world were not already thoroughly familiar with? You claim to expand our horizons, but in fact you shrink them.

MACHIAVELLI: Oh, I may have oversimplified a bit. But it is a matter of proportion: I say man is mainly bad; you say he is mainly good. But I maintain that good men are the exception and that in the average man, who is neither a criminal nor a saint, goodness is small and weak and more easily overcome by evil than evil is overcome by goodness.

SOCRATES: You say man is at least mainly bad—

MACHIAVELLI: Yes.

SOCRATES: You make that judgment. By what standard?

MACHIAVELLI: As I said before, Socrates, by my observation of actual human behavior, both firsthand, in my own time, and secondhand, from my extensive reading of man's history.

SOCRATES: I did not make my question clear. I do not now ask about your sources of information, your "data base", but about the standard you use to judge this data. When we call anything evil, we all mean that it violates a standard or fails to come up to a standard of some sort, do we not?

MACHIAVELLI: Of course.

SOCRATES: And is that standard itself evil or good or neither? Which of these three shall we say?

MACHIAVELLI: I'm not sure I understand what you mean by that question, Socrates.

SOCRATES: Well, come and consider along with me: If the standard for judging anything evil were itself evil, how could that be a valid standard? Surely the ignorant cannot judge ignorance by standards that are ignorant.

MACHIAVELLI: Obviously.

SOCRATES: Well, then, what if this standard is neither evil nor good? For instance, what if we judge whether or not it is evil for a rich man to attain the end of becoming a bishop by means of giving the pope a large sum of money to buy that office—I believe the Church calls that practice "simony"—what if we judge whether or not simony is evil by the standard of whether the money is shiny or dull or whether the coins are Italian or not? This standard is not a matter of good or evil, is it?

MACHIAVELLI: No.

SOCRATES: Can we judge whether or not a thing is evil by such a standard?

MACHIAVELLI: No.

SOCRATES: Then it remains that we must use a standard of goodness, not of evil or of what is neither good nor evil.

MACHIAVELLI: Yes.

SOCRATES: And to use a standard, to judge by it, we must know it?

MACHIAVELLI: Of course.

SOCRATES: So in order to judge that man is evil, you must know the good—the good that man does not achieve, though he should.

MACHIAVELLI: Yes.

SOCRATES: Is this partial goodness or total goodness?

MACHIAVELLI: I don't know . . . I am frankly impatient with this kind of abstract argument.

SOCRATES: Then let us look at concrete facts. Have you ever been a student in school?

MACHIAVELLI: Yes.

SOCRATES: And have you and your classmates ever been tested and judged by your teacher?

MACHIAVELLI: Of course.

SOCRATES: Suppose the teacher gave you a test in mathematics, with ten questions. And suppose you got seven of the ten questions right, while your friend got eight questions right. Would your teacher judge your answers by the standard of your friend?

MACHIAVELLI: No.

SOCRATES: So the standard is not 80 percent but 100 percent?

MACHIAVELLI: Yes.

SOCRATES: Which is a perfect score.

MACHIAVELLI: Yes.

SOCRATES: Shall we look at other examples? Or do you agree that the standard for judging how good or how bad anything is, is always perfect goodness?

MACHIAVELLI: That is the meaning of a standard of judgment in our minds, when we judge. But in the real world we cannot expect anyone to be perfect, so we lower our standards. Shall we look at some examples of this?

SOCRATES: No, I agree that this is what we usually do. And you have agreed that we know, in the mind, a perfect standard when we judge how imperfect a thing is. So when you say man is bad, you know the standard you use: perfect goodness.

MACHIAVELLI: That seems to follow. So what?

SOCRATES: Did you ever experience perfect goodness, in yourself or in others?

MACHIAVELLI: Certainly not!

SOCRATES: You never found it in your study of history or in your own time and culture?

MACHIAVELLI: Never. That is my point: *All* men are bad, some more than others.

SOCRATES: And you claim that all your knowledge is derived from experience, do you not? Or do you believe that your mind can, without experience and the senses, directly know some truth that is eternal and unchangeable and certain?

MACHIAVELLI: I think *you* believe that, Socrates, but I do not.

SOCRATES: Then how do you know perfect goodness?

MACHIAVELLI: It's not a reality; it's just an idea.

SOCRATES: Is it *true*? Suppose I say that perfect human goodness is "to weigh as much as a horse", and you say I am wrong. Is one of us right? Does one of us speak the truth?

MACHIAVELLI: Yes. I do.

SOCRATES: So we can know the truth about perfect goodness.

MACHIAVELLI: I am not convinced of that.

SOCRATES: If we cannot, how can we truly judge of false ideas about it, such as my confusing it with the weight of a horse? Remember the case of the teacher grading the students.

MACHIAVELLI: All right, so we know an ideal standard, and we know that no man attains it, that all men are bad, as I said. So what? What are you getting at?

SOCRATES: Do you not see the implications of your philosophy of man in your epistemology and your metaphysics?

MACHIAVELLI: I avoided those impractical subjects, Socrates.

SOCRATES: But you can't. If, as you say, you truly know that man is bad, then it logically follows that your knowledge is not limited to experience and that truth is not limited to the imperfect but also includes a real standard that we have called perfect goodness.

MACHIAVELLI: I never claimed to be a philosopher, Socrates. My book is not about such questions, and I think it is unfair of you to demand an answer to them from me. I thought we were supposed to examine the book I wrote, not the book I failed to write.

SOCRATES: Then let us return to your book.

8

The Power of Trust

SOCRATES: Would you say that being the head of a state—a prince—resembles in many ways being the head of a business?

MACHIAVELLI: Yes. And the reader can find much practical advice about how to run both in my book. Of course, there are differences, too: for instance, it is wealth that empowers a business, while it is arms that empower a state.

SOCRATES: Would you say that the piece of advice you give at the end of chapter 3 applies to a business as well as a state? You write,

Wootten, p. 14, ll. 18–21.
From this one can draw a general conclusion that will never (or hardly ever) be proved wrong: He who is the cause of someone else's becoming powerful is the agent of his own destruction.

MACHIAVELLI: Yes. Both businesses and states work by constant rivalry—as you would know if you had had any real experience of either.

SOCRATES: Also in the same chapter, you advise a prince to reside in newly conquered territories himself, as the Turks did in Greece, because in this way,

"the territory will not be plundered by your offi- Wootten, p.
cials". 9, ll. 18–19.

MACHIAVELLI: Yes.

SOCRATES: So you advise the prince to trust no one.

MACHIAVELLI: Yes. This logically follows from the principle that all men are wicked.

SOCRATES: Have you ever heard of the business term "micro-managing"?

MACHIAVELLI: No, but I can imagine what it means: the head of a business must not lose control to his subordinates but must be present to all parts of his business, as a prince should be present in his colonies, lest they rebel or be badly administered.

SOCRATES: And you consider this good practical advice?

MACHIAVELLI: Certainly.

SOCRATES: Not to trust your subordinates?

MACHIAVELLI: Yes.

SOCRATES: But what could possibly be *less* practical? Consider the time, the worry, the energy, and even the money that you could save if you could generate mutual trust throughout your realm. Consider also how your principle *limits* your power—

MACHIAVELLI: Now this interests me!

SOCRATES: You might be able to "micro-manage" a small business successfully, or a small state; but the greater the extent of your dominion, and the more you wish to expand your empire and thus your power, the more impossible it will become. You might keep constant check on twenty employees, but you cannot personally check on twenty thousand. For that, you need subordinates you can trust. The greater your power, the more it must work by trust rather than mistrust.

MACHIAVELLI: I admit this is a problem, Socrates, but if all men are bad and *not* trustworthy, I see no workable solution to it.

SOCRATES: My case rests. Now let us look at a wider application of this principle of mistrust: your reliance on fear and force, that is, arms.

MACHIAVELLI: Ah, I knew you would bring that up. You are taking aim already, I see, at my infamous principle that "it is better to be feared than loved", aren't you? That is what shocks all my readers at first. But consider the alternative: Do you want to run a state on love? And an army? And a police force? It cannot be done, and it never has been done, and that fact is powerful proof of my philosophy of man, that men are fundamentally bad: selfish and competitive.

SOCRATES: Well, let's look at what you actually said.

MACHIAVELLI: Thank you. I will stand by it, I assure you.

9

Arms and Laws

SOCRATES: Let us begin with something very specific and concrete: your military advice in *The Prince*.

MACHIAVELLI: My most solid ground, I believe.

SOCRATES: You praise the Romans, in chapter 3, **"for they knew that wars cannot be avoided and can only be deferred to the advantage of others."** Donno, p. 18, ll. 24–25.

MACHIAVELLI: Yes.

SOCRATES: You don't mean only *"should* not be avoided" but *"cannot* be avoided", correct?

MACHIAVELLI: Correct.

SOCRATES: Perhaps you *are* correct about some wars. But do you say that *no* wars are avoidable? Are there no examples in history of peace treaties and alliances that have been mutually profitable? How could war be more profitable than peace? Peace preserves, and war destroys, much of the wealth, manpower, and artifacts of both warring nations.

MACHIAVELLI: Of course it does. But men are wicked, remember? They prefer war to peace. Peace bores them. All men lust for victory and glory.

SOCRATES: If that is true, then I am not a man, for I do not lust for these things.

MACHIAVELLI: Hmm—perhaps that would explain many strange things about you, Socrates.

SOCRATES: But I assure you I am a man. I can show you my parents as proof. But not now.

MACHIAVELLI: I was kidding, Socrates.

SOCRATES: You can kid me, Niccolò, but you cannot kid a syllogism. You must answer it.

MACHIAVELLI: All right, perhaps I shall admit that some men do not lust for victory. But most do. And the most successful men in history, the Romans, taught us how to attain it, if we would only learn from their irrefutable example. I always find concrete examples more irrefutable than abstract principles or arguments. You can't argue with success.

SOCRATES: And therefore you say in your fourteenth chapter, on the art of war: **"A ruler, then, should have no other concern, no other thought, should pay attention to nothing aside from war, military institutions, and the training of his soldiers. For this is the only field in which a ruler has to excel."** And later in the same chapter you say, **"So a ruler must think only of military matters, and in time of peace he should be even more occupied with them."**

Wootton, p. 45, ll. 31–34, p. 46, ll. 20–21.

Is this not another great inefficiency for one who seeks power and wants to be practical? Suppose you could attain all the ends for which you fight a war *without* the loss of lives and weapons and time and energy and wealth—would that not increase your power? If you could capture a fort or a queen or a ship or the wealth of a people with a hundred soldiers, would it not be folly and inefficiency to use a thousand?

MACHIAVELLI: Yes.

SOCRATES: But what if one soldier could do it? Would it not be folly to send a hundred?

MACHIAVELLI: Of course. But one will never do.

SOCRATES: But what if none would do? What if you could attain war's end without war at all?

MACHIAVELLI: You can't.

SOCRATES: At no time? By no means? Does history show no such examples?

MACHIAVELLI: No! I know what you are about to say, Socrates: the classical argument that the end of war is peace, or a certain kind of peace; and then you will say that *sometimes* only war can attain this end, but sometimes diplomacy or persuasion or a mutual enemy or an assassination or a political coup has worked. But I say that man is restless without war and that the end sought by war is *not* peace but conquest and glory; and that this process must continue, like a living body killing and eating food, and that this is the law of man's nature, which ceases only in death.

SOCRATES: So war must continue and expand forever.

MACHIAVELLI: Until there are no more worlds to conquer. Alexander was never defeated by war; he was only defeated by peace. And Rome was healthy and growing when her empire was expanding by conquest; but when only barbarians and Persians remained outside her frontiers and the *pax romana* ensued, she began to decline, like an old man who retires from fulltime athletic competition and gets fat.

SOCRATES: And what is the end and goal and purpose of all this conquest by war?

MACHIAVELLI: Why, victory, of course.

SOCRATES: But that is just another name for conquest. What do you—what do we all, according to you—seek victory or conquest *for*?

MACHIAVELLI: What a silly question, Socrates! Everyone wants victory, as everyone wants life. No one wants defeat.

SOCRATES: Of course, this is true—of most men, anyway. (I wonder what the women would say about that, by the way?)

MACHIAVELLI: Oh, please Socrates! Surely we are not required to descend so low as to become the pupils of women!

SOCRATES: I will not reply to that because it would shock you and also would lead us into a very long diversion, perhaps an endless one. You say, then, that victory, like life, is its own end?

MACHIAVELLI: Yes.

SOCRATES: So do you say also that the question of the meaning of life, the purpose of life, the final end of life, the *summum bonum*, or greatest good—that this is a foolish question, since life has no end and purpose but is itself its own end and purpose?

MACHIAVELLI: Why may I not say that if I will?

SOCRATES: Because if life were itself the highest good, then to risk it or to sacrifice it in war would be folly, not glory and honor. And that would be a coward's philosophy.

MACHIAVELLI: Then I will reject it.

SOCRATES: Then you must say that life, and also victory, to which you compared it, is not its own end but *has* some end or purpose.

MACHIAVELLI: Yes, I shall say that.

SOCRATES: I think you can guess my next question.

MACHIAVELLI: You will ask me what it is.

SOCRATES: Yes.

MACHIAVELLI: Socrates, you amaze me. You begin with a nice, concrete question about princes and armies, and then you twist it into the airiest of abstractions, and we are soon flying like angels discussing the *summum bonum*! You, you—

SOCRATES: Niccolò!

MACHIAVELLI: What?

SOCRATES: You haven't answered the question.

MACHIAVELLI: That's because I don't believe I have to.

SOCRATES: And why is that?

MACHIAVELLI: Because the question of "the greatest good" is a question about goods and morals and ideals. And what determines good and evil in any state is simply its laws. And the laws in any state are made by those who have the power to make laws. And that power was attained by force of arms. I go immediately to the real cause, Socrates, while you muddle around in the later effect. That is why you get nowhere, like a child chasing shadows. I talk about arms, because there lies the real root and cause of the power to make the laws that define the good. I know you do not agree with my philosophy, but surely you must admire my logic.

SOCRATES: I cannot admire what I do not first see. Let us try to see your logic, close up and literal. Here is the passage where you justify your advice to the prince to be obsessed with arms. It is in the twelfth chapter: **"We said above that a prince must build on sound foundations; otherwise he is bound to come to grief."** [Certainly sound advice thus far!] **"The main foundations of every state . . . are good laws and good arms; and because you cannot have good laws without good arms, and where there are good arms, good laws inevitably follow, I shall not discuss laws but give my attention to arms."**

Bull, p. 77, ll. 8–15.

Your last sentence logically depends on everything before it, especially what immediately precedes: If it is true that **"where there are good arms, good laws inevitably follow"**, then it is wise and practical to discuss arms, not laws, because, as you say in your first sentence, *foundations* must be well laid. And if arms are the sole foundations of states, we must attend to them solely; and if they are the chief foundations (even if not the sole foundations), we must attend to them chiefly (even if not solely).

MACHIAVELLI: So you see and admire my logic, Socrates. And since you also admire my premise, about foundations, as you said, you must, logically, admire my conclusion. This science of yours, logic, compels you to admire this science of mine, practical politics.

SOCRATES: Let us not be too hasty.

MACHIAVELLI: But you have agreed with both the truth of my premise and the validity of the logic by which my conclusion follows.

SOCRATES: Yes, but we have not examined the middle links in your chain of reasoning. A chain is no stronger than its weakest link, you know.

MACHIAVELLI: There is no weak link, I assure you.

SOCRATES: Now it is I who refuse to trust and who insist on proof, not assurances. Let me see—here is the passage: **"You cannot have good laws without good arms, and where there are good arms, good laws inevitably follow."**

MACHIAVELLI: Well?

SOCRATES: These two statements—that **"you cannot have good laws without good arms"** and that **"where there are good arms, good laws inevitably follow"**—do you claim that they are logically equivalent?

MACHIAVELLI: Sounds right to me.

SOCRATES: Suppose I say, first, that you cannot have a sword fight without a sword, and second, that where there is a sword, a sword fight inevitably follows. Do you say these two statements are logically equivalent?

MACHIAVELLI: They are both true, if that's what you mean.

SOCRATES: No, that is not what I mean. I mean: Do you claim that either one can be deduced from the other?

MACHIAVELLI: I don't put much stock in deduction, Socrates. I claim they are both known to be true by induction, from repeated observation.

SOCRATES: Do you understand the difference between a *sufficient* cause and a *necessary* cause?

MACHIAVELLI: Of course. A father is a necessary cause of a son, but not a sufficient cause, since a mother is also needed.

SOCRATES: Good. Now look at your first statement: **"You cannot have good laws without good arms."** You are claiming that good arms are a *necessary* cause of good laws, are you not?

MACHIAVELLI: Yes.

SOCRATES: But in your second statement, **"where there are good arms, good laws inevitably follow"**, you are claiming that good arms are a sufficient cause of good laws.

MACHIAVELLI: Yes. And both claims are true, though the second claims more.

SOCRATES: And therefore is more likely to be false —as with my example of the sword and the sword fight. A sword *is* a necessary cause of a sword fight, of course, but it is not a sufficient cause. You need a man to wield it, too.

MACHIAVELLI: Of course.

SOCRATES: And perhaps your second statement about arms and laws is also false. It does not logically follow from the first one. So we must use observation to test its truth.

MACHIAVELLI: Exactly what I have done.

SOCRATES: But you have not done it correctly. You have forgotten some facts. History shows that inventors of good laws have only sometimes been armed, like the Romans and Napoleon, but sometimes not, like Moses, Hammurabi, Confucius, Jesus, and the American Constitutional Convention.

MACHIAVELLI: The *what*?

SOCRATES: Oh, yes. You would not know about that.

MACHIAVELLI: Can you tell me?

SOCRATES: I will tell you this: that almost three centuries after you died the best set of laws in history formed a great nation named after your friend Amerigo Vespucci.

MACHIAVELLI: Then as my excuse, I plead ignorance of this new history that you know. I am only a man, not a god, after all.

SOCRATES: Oh, there is no obstacle to excusing *you*. Your person and motives are not on trial here. And if they were, I certainly could not be your judge. But it is your book that is on trial.

MACHIAVELLI: I understand.

SOCRATES: Then when you plead the excuse of personal ignorance, you admit that there is something in your book that needs an excuse.

MACHIAVELLI: I admitted that, I think.

SOCRATES: Does truth need an excuse, or does falsehood?

MACHIAVELLI: Falsehood, of course.

SOCRATES: I rest my case.

MACHIAVELLI: But how could I know the future?

SOCRATES: Moses, Hammurabi, Confucius, Jesus— were they future to you?

MACHIAVELLI: No, they were past history.

SOCRATES: Then you are refuted by past history, in which you claimed to be an expert.

10

Love and Fear

MACHIAVELLI: Which of my little soldiers will be struck next by your grapeshot?

SOCRATES: My questions are not like grapeshot, for grapeshot is projected at random from the gun.

MACHIAVELLI: Well, you certainly seem to be doing that. You said you would first examine my anthropology and only then my ethics and metaphysics and epistemology and logic, none of which I claimed to teach anyway. But you have led us into those questions already, all of them, while you were supposed to be exploring only my anthropology.

SOCRATES: I couldn't help it. I must follow the argument wherever it leads. And it has led us, and no doubt will continue to lead, into all of these aspects of philosophy, like streets in a city. Neither the logic of the argument nor my following it is random.

MACHIAVELLI: But our focus is to be on my philosophy of man, for that is the focus of my book.

SOCRATES: Correct. And on its central principle, from which nearly everything else in your book follows, which seems to be the principle that all men are bad.

MACHIAVELLI: You will claim, no doubt, that all my conclusions are deduced from this principle rather than induced from history, as I claim they are. You do not seem to have taken seriously my claim that I am not a philosopher but a scientist, and I justify my conclusions, not by deduction, but by induction.

SOCRATES: I only follow what you yourself have written; and you explicitly deduce the conclusion I now want to examine from this fundamental principle of yours.

MACHIAVELLI: What conclusion?

SOCRATES: That it is better to be feared than to be loved.

MACHIAVELLI: I knew you'd direct your attention to that eventually.

SOCRATES: Of course you did: that is why you wrote it. "Shock value", I think it is called. But that is only my guess, and I am not here to analyze your motives but your words. Here they are—probably the most famous passage you ever wrote—

MACHIAVELLI: Before you go on, could you just satisfy my historian's curiosity about something?

SOCRATES: Not if it is a diversion from this passage.

MACHIAVELLI: It is not. It is about this passage.

SOCRATES: What's the question?

MACHIAVELLI: Well, you seem to know many facts of history that happened long after you died, including events in my own lifetime, for instance those surrounding Fra Savonarola, and even things afterward. Tell me, did this saying of mine really become famous?

SOCRATES: Infamous, yes.

MACHIAVELLI: Among the people at large?

SOCRATES: Somewhat. For example, it was the main theme of a movie called *A Bronx Tale*.

MACHIAVELLI: What's a "movie"?

SOCRATES: We have no time for that now. We must return to our serious work. We must examine your words in chapter 17:

> **This leads us to a question that is in dispute: Is it better to be loved than feared, or vice versa? My reply is one ought to be both loved and feared; but, since it is difficult to accomplish both at the same time, I maintain it is much safer to be feared than loved, if you have to do without one of the two. For of men one can, in general, say this: They are ungrateful, fickle, deceptive and deceiving, avoiders of danger, eager to gain. As long as you serve their interests, they are devoted to you. They promise you their blood, their possessions, their lives, and their children, as I said before, so long as you seem to have no need of them. But as soon as you need help, they turn against you. . . . Men are less nervous of offending someone who makes himself lovable, than someone who makes himself frightening. For love attaches men**

by ties of obligation, which, since men are wicked, they break whenever their interests are at stake. But fear restrains men because they are afraid of punishment, and this fear never leaves them. . . .

I conclude, then, that, as far as being feared and loved is concerned, since men decide for themselves whom they love, and rulers decide whom they fear, a wise ruler should rely on the emotion he can control, not on the one he cannot.

Wootton, p. 51, ll. 31–34; p. 52, ll. 1–6, 12–16; p. 53, ll. 23–26.

I congratulate you on your brilliant clarity and literary style, by the way. It makes my task of logical analysis of the truth or falsity of what you say much easier.

Now regarding what you say here—

MACHIAVELLI: But I also say, in the very next sentence, **"Still, a ruler should make himself feared in such a way that, if he does not inspire love, at least he does not provoke hatred."**

Wootton, p. 52, ll. 17–18.

SOCRATES: Yes, but that does not change what you said before.

MACHIAVELLI: I know this passage must be morally shocking to you, but it is not about morality. It is typical of the whole book: I do not claim to tell men what they should or should not do, only what policies will work. *The Prince* is practice, not theory, and politics, not ethics.

SOCRATES: Oh, I understand that. My question about this passage is not whether it is ethical but whether it is practical.

MACHIAVELLI: Good. And let us not get too much into philosophical theory, then.

SOCRATES: But we must do *that*. For *you* do! You deduce your practical conclusion from a general theory about man. You explicitly say that: **"For of men one can, in general, say this: They are ungrateful"**, and so on. And again, you say, **"love attaches men by ties of obligation, which, *since men are wicked*, they break."**

MACHIAVELLI: But that premise is not theory; it is fact. My general principles are like scientific formulas: they are based on observation—many observations, aided by the instruments of history; and they lead to practical conclusions, practical applications—political technology, you might say.

SOCRATES: I understand that. But if for any reasons your formula—your premise or principle—is *not* a fact, is false or half false, then your practical applications of it—your political technology—will fail. If your theory fails, your practice that is based on it will fail too.

MACHIAVELLI: And *I* understand *that*.

SOCRATES: So you do *not* avoid theory or general principles or deduction.

MACHIAVELLI: No, but my aim is practice, not theory. And I begin and end with particulars, not generalities. I begin with particular observations; I derive general principles from them; and, then, apply my principles to particular practice.

SOCRATES: So it is perfectly fair to examine the general principle or formula that connects your initial observations with your final practical applications, to see whether this general principle may not be the weak link in your chain. Do you claim your formulas are immune from such critique?

MACHIAVELLI: No, of course not.

SOCRATES: Then let us proceed, since we have agreed on the logical rules. Tell me, please, how great and varied are the observations of human behavior on which you base your general principle that all men are bad?

MACHIAVELLI: As wide as the world and as varied as history.

SOCRATES: And nowhere in the world have you found good men? Are you like Diogenes the Cynic, who dressed only in a barrel and brought a lantern into the marketplace looking in vain for an honest man?

MACHIAVELLI: I have no barrel and no lantern, but I have no more faith in humanity than Diogenes had. *You* should understand my disillusionment, Socrates; didn't you spend a lifetime looking for a wise man in vain?

SOCRATES: That is not the same. For one thing, I found that there could be many wise men; for anyone who knows he is not wise is wise. But as for goodness, do you say there is none in mankind or little? Would you deny even "honor among thieves"? Or that some men are worse than others, and therefore some are better and have *some* good, at least, mixed with the evil in them?

MACHIAVELLI: Little, then.

SOCRATES: *How* little? How shall we measure it? And how take account of the good, little as it may be, and the effects it will have on behavior? You ignored this in your book, and I wonder how can that be practical? How can you call yourself a realist if you ignore any part of reality?

MACHIAVELLI: I admitted there is a little good in man. But I maintain that his evil is far stronger, especially when you need to deal with man as a successful prince does. I do not claim to solve the question children and philosophers idly argue in the comforts of the playroom or the classroom, the question about how much good there is in man and how much evil. I leave that to the philosophers. I answer a different question: I tell a prospective prince how to control human behavior.

SOCRATES: Then I think you will be very interested in something that scientists discovered five centuries after your time. These were scientists of human behavior, not philosophers; and most of them were atheists, skeptics, and materialists. They called themselves "behaviorists" because they were interested only in changing human behavior in practice. They discovered that love of rewards works more effectively than fear of punishment in altering and controlling human behavior. Does that surprise you?

MACHIAVELLI: Indeed, it does. Unless men in that century somehow changed their nature and became gentle and civilized.

SOCRATES: No, alas. In fact, that century witnessed the most massive state-organized murders in history. (They called them "genocides".)

MACHIAVELLI: How many victims were there?

SOCRATES: More than a hundred million.

MACHIAVELLI: So human nature did not change.

SOCRATES: No. And yet most men responded better to good than to evil, to love than to fear.

MACHIAVELLI: I do not understand how that could possibly be. But you have an inductive argument for love, while I had a *deductive* argument for fear. And a deductive argument is more certain than an inductive one.

SOCRATES: How interesting that we are exchanging our positions on logical method to preserve our positions on love versus fear. What is your deductive argument?

MACHIAVELLI: In my last paragraph, I argue that the love that others have for you is controlled by their will, not yours, so it is to you part of *fortuna*; while their fear of you is controlled by your will, not theirs, so it is to you part of *virtù*. Thus the principle of success, to maximize *virtù* and minimize *fortuna*, justifies my conclusion that you should rely more on fear than on love.

SOCRATES: What you will is under your control, is it not?

MACHIAVELLI: Yes.

SOCRATES: And thus comes under *virtù*?

MACHIAVELLI: Yes.

SOCRATES: But the things others choose to do to you come from *their* will, do they not?

MACHIAVELLI: Yes.

SOCRATES: And thus come under *fortuna*.

MACHIAVELLI: To you, yes.

SOCRATES: And you reject the "Golden Rule", which tells you to do to others the good that you would want them to do to you?

MACHIAVELLI: Yes. That is a good rule for sheep, but not for wolves or princes.

SOCRATES: Instead, you justify doing to others the harm they would do to you.

MACHIAVELLI: Yes. That is my principle of success.

SOCRATES: So your principle is not "Do unto others what you would want them to do unto you", but "Do unto others what they would do unto you"—but do it first.

MACHIAVELLI: Ha! ha! That is a nice way of putting it, Socrates. I like that.

SOCRATES: And what you will is *virtù*, but what you do not will is *fortuna*.

MACHIAVELLI: Yes.

SOCRATES: And the harm others want to do to you is *fortuna*, not *virtù*, to you?

MACHIAVELLI: Yes.

SOCRATES: Then your rule is to act according to *their* will, which is *fortuna*, and not according to *your* will, which is *virtù*. Does that not violate your general principle for success, which is to maximize *virtù* and minimize *fortuna*?

MACHIAVELLI: I don't know how your twisted logic came up with that conclusion, Socrates.

SOCRATES: Oh, I think you do. The logic was neither twisted nor terribly difficult, especially to a man of your intelligence.

MACHIAVELLI: But I don't *want* the Golden Rule, which is justice and equality. And I certainly don't want to live by love and charity. I want my own freedom and power to do as I will; and I maintain that every man wants this too, but I show the way to get it.

SOCRATES: I know an easier way to get it.

MACHIAVELLI: So you acknowledge that all men want it?

SOCRATES: Freedom and power to do what we will? Of course we all want that. Who wants to be enslaved or impotent and frustrated?

MACHIAVELLI: Well, then, what is your "easier way" to get it?

SOCRATES: Love. If you want the conquest of *fortuna* by *virtù*, why not live a life of love?

MACHIAVELLI: That's ridiculous. Love is free, so others will love you as *they* will, not as you will. That life is maximal dependence on *fortuna*, not *virtù*.

SOCRATES: Not if what you want is to *love* rather than to *be* loved. You yourself said that **"men decide for themselves whom they love"**. So the way to live in total freedom and power, always getting what you will and not being dependent on *fortuna*, is to live a life of loving. For to love *is* always in your power.

MACHIAVELLI: This is ridiculous. Fear is stronger than love, far stronger.

SOCRATES: Is it? What happens when love enters a life that was previously dominated by fear? Does not love cast out fear?

MACHIAVELLI: I do not enforce my will by loving, but by the sword, which controls men!

SOCRATES: And those who live by the sword usually perish by the sword, do they not? Come now, Niccolò, you are a realist and a man of the world; you know that is true.

MACHIAVELLI: I can't believe this! You are claiming that the saint is more powerful than the tyrant who kills him—and you dare to suggest to a worldly man like myself that this is realistic and practical?

SOCRATES: Why not? Many have tested it in practice and in real life.

MACHIAVELLI: But the Golden Rule, the life of justice, and the life of charity that exceeds it, are for private persons who wish to become saints. They are not for politics. Show me a state run by charity. Show me a state run by saints!

SOCRATES: So you believe there must be a double standard, one for private and one for public, one for saints and one for princes.

MACHIAVELLI: Of course, unless you want me to identify religion and politics!

SOCRATES: So the ruler must follow a very different rule from the one he wants his citizens to follow, almost the opposite rule?

MACHIAVELLI: Certainly. For if all his citizens were as wise and unscrupulous as the ruler, he would find effective rule to be very difficult. He wants to keep his people quiet, like sheep, while he himself is like a wolf.

SOCRATES: The ruler is a human being, is he not?

MACHIAVELLI: Of course.

SOCRATES: As are all his citizens?

MACHIAVELLI: Of course.

SOCRATES: So they are not members of two species like wolf and sheep, but one?

MACHIAVELLI: Of course. It was only a metaphor.

SOCRATES: And the members of any species all share the same essential nature, do they not?

MACHIAVELLI: That is true by definition.

SOCRATES: So whatever principles of human nature you rely on in advising the ruler are also possessed by each of his citizens?

MACHIAVELLI: Yes.

SOCRATES: And they therefore *could* act as he acts, though a sheep could never act like a wolf.

MACHIAVELLI: Well, yes, in theory—

SOCRATES: And whatever principles of human nature the ruler recognizes in his citizens and tries to manipulate in controlling them exist in himself as well, do they not?

MACHIAVELLI: Yes. It is power, not nature, that enables him to be a ruler and prevents his flock from being so. They are equal in nature but unequal in power and cleverness.

SOCRATES: But you say that *all* men are bad, therefore all are justified in being distrustful; and you say that *all* who wish to be wise and successful must use fear more than love. Now this advice is based on human nature in general, is it not?

MACHIAVELLI: Yes.

SOCRATES: So it is only ignorance on the part of the sheep, and not a lack of anything common to human nature, that keeps them sheep; and it is only the knowledge you teach in your book that enables the ruler to rise above the sheep and be like a wolf.

MACHIAVELLI: Yes. My book is the key to power. Knowledge is power. You taught that knowledge was *virtue*—moral virtue, sheepish virtue. I teach that knowledge is *virtù*—wolfish virtue, power.

SOCRATES: So if your book got into the wrong hands, it would be self-defeating. It would teach the sheep how to become wolves.

MACHIAVELLI: Well, yes, under certain conditions—

SOCRATES: Why, then, did you publish it? Why do you seek fame? Why do you share your power, which is your knowledge? Why do you act like one who obeys the Golden Rule?

MACHIAVELLI: Hmmm. Perhaps deep down I am a saint.

SOCRATES: That is certainly not for me to decide. But in the saints I have met—a very wide spectrum of humanity, by the way—I have observed many human foibles and weaknesses and even murderous rage at times, but never once the thing I see now and often on your face, Niccolò Machiavelli.

MACHIAVELLI: And what may that be, may I ask, that appears to your outer eye as the inner mark of Cain?

SOCRATES: A sneer.

11

Machiavelli's Ethics

SOCRATES: Still there, Niccolò?

MACHIAVELLI: After that low blow, why should I stay?

SOCRATES: Why do you call it low?

MACHIAVELLI: Because it was not an objective logical argument, which is what I thought your job was here. It was more like—

SOCRATES: Like a sneer?

MACHIAVELLI: A sneer does not fit your face, Socrates.

SOCRATES: Only yours?

MACHIAVELLI: Well, yes. But you are supposed to be pure logic incarnate, without personal tricks.

SOCRATES: Is it a trick to make an accurate description of another's face? Is a mirror a "personal trick"?

MACHIAVELLI: I thought you were here to examine my book, not me.

SOCRATES: Correct. The latter task can be carried out only by two, and I am not one of them.

MACHIAVELLI: Two? Who?

SOCRATES: Why, the only two whom you can never escape, to all eternity.

MACHIAVELLI: God, you mean? I'll take my own chances there, thank you. But who else?

SOCRATES: Yourself. But you are right: we should be examining your book. Shall we review what we have found so far?

MACHIAVELLI: I think I do not have much choice.

SOCRATES: We have been evaluating your philosophy of man by your own standards, to see whether it is realistic and practical. We have discovered that you deduce many of your practical conclusions from the principle that all men are bad. Thus you discount many things previous thinkers took very serious account of: the common good, the moral force of conscience, the power of a saint with no arms, trust in your friends, and love. It seems that you are neglecting much in human nature—thus *not* being realistic or true to reality. On the other hand, the things you do emphasize—fear, force of arms, and human wickedness in many forms, which are indeed real— not one single true observation you have made about them has been unknown to the ancients, to the old moralists like myself and Moses and Solomon and Jesus and Muhammad and Confucius and Buddha and Lao-Tzu.

That is my summary of what I have found so far. And it puzzles me how such a *contraction* of the horizon could appear to anyone as a bold, new *expansion* of horizons. You say you will teach us how to be bad, where the ancients had only taught us how to be good. But we have always known how to be bad. By your own account this is true, for you say all men are wicked.

MACHIAVELLI: Hmph!

SOCRATES: Is *that* your answer to these charges? "Hmph"?

MACHIAVELLI: My answer is in my particular advice. Your charges are all abstract and general. I thought you were going to examine what I actually wrote, in detail.

SOCRATES: That is exactly what I am doing. So let's see exactly what you say about good and evil, **"those factors that cause men . . . to be praised or censured"**, to use your formula and chapter title. Chapter 15, I think.

Wootton, p. 47, ll. 33–34.

MACHIAVELLI: Examine away, then.

SOCRATES: There is a passage about this same topic earlier, in chapter 3, that is revealing, too; let me quote that first:

The wish to acquire more is admittedly a very natural and common thing; and when men succeed in this they are always praised rather than condemned. But when they lack the ability to do so and yet want to acquire more at all costs, they deserve condemnation for their mistakes. If France could have attacked Naples with her own forces, she should have done so; if not, she should not have divided it.

Bull, p. 42, ll. 11–18.

MACHIAVELLI: I hope you understand that this **"should"** is not the "should" of moral obligation but of practical advice.

SOCRATES: That is what I thought you were up to *until* I read this passage.

MACHIAVELLI: I don't understand why this passage led you to interpret—to misinterpret—my advice as moral rather than practical. I was speaking of military strategy in this chapter, remember?

SOCRATES: You clearly distinguish two "shoulds" or "oughts", then: the moral and the practical?

MACHIAVELLI: Yes.

SOCRATES: And what do you mean by each?

MACHIAVELLI: The practical "ought" is what works, what is effective, what attains your end, *whatever* your end is, whether that end is thought to be morally good or evil or neutral. And this practical "ought" is an objective fact that we can discover by the methods of science, and thus we can resolve disputes about it. For instance, iron is better in a shield than copper; Egypt did not know this and lost a war to Assyria because of it. If I were advising the ruler of Egypt, I would say he "ought" to get iron, make shields of it, and put off the war against Syria until he does.

SOCRATES: That is very clear. Now what is the moral "ought"?

MACHIAVELLI: The moral "ought" cannot be settled by science, and men have argued about moral good and evil forever without resolving these disputes. The reason is that the moral "ought" is imposed by conscience, which is not an objective fact but a subjective feeling, and different individuals and different societies have different feelings about what is moral and what is not. For instance, suicide, infanticide, abortion, and sodomy were all felt to be honorable by many in pre-Christian Greek or Roman society, but all of these practices are felt to be dishonorable and evil by Christian consciences and societies.

SOCRATES: Whether this account of moral good and evil as a subjective thing is correct or not is too large a question for us to discuss now, though I hope to do so later. But it suffices that you distinguish it from the practical good as you do.

Now in light of your distinction, you claim that in the passage I read you speak only of the practical good, or the practical "ought", and not the moral. Is that correct?

MACHIAVELLI: It is.

SOCRATES: Then let us examine exactly what you are saying and just how practical it is.

MACHIAVELLI: That is the fair question, Socrates; thank you for not criticizing me for a lack of morality that I did not mean to have or express.

SOCRATES: Tell me, if you were a general and someone informed you of the fact that the general who opposes you in war is a drunkard who never wakes up sober until an hour after sunrise, would that information be of practical use?

MACHIAVELLI: Of course. That information could enable me to defeat him by attacking at dawn.

SOCRATES: And if someone informed you of the fact that the general who opposes you is the general who opposes you, would that be of practical use?

MACHIAVELLI: Of course not. Those empty words give me no information at all.

SOCRATES: Logicians call such empty words a *tautology*: the predicate adds nothing at all to the subject.

MACHIAVELLI: What does this have to do with the passage we are discussing in my book?

SOCRATES: Patience, please. We will see the connection very shortly. Now suppose I said that the general who opposes you in war is the highest military commander of the army that stands against you in military conflict.

MACHIAVELLI: That also gives me no information, only new words, mere synonyms for the old ones. The predicate merely repeats the subject in different words.

SOCRATES: And such tautologies are never of practical use, are they?

MACHIAVELLI: No.

SOCRATES: Now let us see whether you have given us something practical or a mere tautology. You say that when men lack the ability to acquire what they want **"and yet want to acquire more at all costs, they deserve condemnation."**

MACHIAVELLI: Yes.

SOCRATES: And **"If France *could* have attacked Naples with her own forces, she *should* have done so."**

MACHIAVELLI: Yes.

SOCRATES: And this is not the moral "should" you say, but the practical one.

MACHIAVELLI: Right.

SOCRATES: So all you are saying is that if France's attack was practical, then it was practical; and that when men will an impractical and unattainable goal, wishing to acquire what they cannot, that this is impractical. For you say that you mean by "ought" only "can" or what works; and by "ought not" only "cannot" or what does not work—the practically bad, not the morally bad. So I do not see how you are saying anything more than a tautology—which is totally *impractical*.

Unless you *are* speaking of a moral good and relating it to the practical good and saying that when a man seeks an end that is practically attainable, he ought not to listen to moral scruples, but that it is perfectly right, morally, to do what is workable, practically. That is what most of your readers thought you meant, and that is why they called you the Devil's son and other uncomplimentary names. (In fact, not only were you named after the Devil, but he was also named "Old Nick" after you, Niccolò!) But you said that these readers had misunderstood you, for you were only speaking of the practical good here.

So you seem to be faced with a dilemma: Are you an immoralist or an impracticalist? The Devil's son or an empty-word-spinner-of-tautologies?

MACHIAVELLI: I would rather be known as the Devil's son than an empty-word-spinner-of-tautologies.

SOCRATES: Would you also rather *be* the Devil's son than an empty-word-spinner-of-tautologies?

MACHIAVELLI: I can't answer that question.

SOCRATES: I will not pursue it. So you say in this passage that if you *can* acquire a thing, you *should*. "Can" implies "ought".

MACHIAVELLI: That formula had a nice sound to it.

SOCRATES: Would you consider this formula as an alternative: "*Ought* implies *can*"? It has just as nice a sound to it, and it is more sound logically, I think.

MACHIAVELLI: "*Ought* implies *can*"—you mean we are morally obliged to do only what is within our power, not outside it?

SOCRATES: Yes, exactly. You put it very well, Niccolò.

MACHIAVELLI: But this is trivially true, a tautology.

SOCRATES: Perhaps not. Are there not some people who feel morally guilty for not doing what they cannot do?

MACHIAVELLI: Yes.

SOCRATES: So this maxim would free them from their guilt.

MACHIAVELLI: Yes.

SOCRATES: That does not seem trivial, then. And are there not some philosophers who claim we have no free will, but are like machines, or that we are wholly victims of fortune?

MACHIAVELLI: Yes.

SOCRATES: So this maxim would refute them, too. And that is not trivial.

MACHIAVELLI: You are right.

SOCRATES: In fact, a few hundred years after you died, a philosopher named Kant used exactly that maxim and that argument to prove free will. Some day I shall examine his book, too. Now let us look at your formula, "*Can* implies *ought*." Do you mean the practical *ought* or the moral *ought*?

MACHIAVELLI: The practical *ought*.

SOCRATES: And what is practical is what is possible, what you *can* do successfully?

MACHIAVELLI: Yes.

SOCRATES: Then "*Can* implies *ought*" means only "*Can* implies *can*." And that is a tautology and *not* a piece of practical information.

MACHIAVELLI: Then *ought* means the moral *ought*.

SOCRATES: So "*Can* implies *ought*" means that you have a moral obligation to do whatever you *can* do.

MACHIAVELLI: Perhaps that is what it means.

SOCRATES: But then it is obviously false. A successful prince *can* surrender his power to incompetent subordinates, but that does not mean he *ought* to—either morally or practically.

MACHIAVELLI: Then the formula does not work, and I repudiate it. For neither empty tautologies nor falsehoods are practical. I will not hold onto an ideology at the expense of practicality.

SOCRATES: Perhaps there is some hope for you yet. We are, after all, still writing your real book, which is not *The Prince* but your life.

MACHIAVELLI: Do you mean that we are *in* a book? Now?

SOCRATES: Yes, indeed. Someone is writing this conversation.

MACHIAVELLI: How strange!

SOCRATES: Not at all. It happened to me before, in Athens.

MACHIAVELLI: Are we then not real, but only literary fictions?

SOCRATES: Of course we are real.

MACHIAVELLI: But you said we are in a book.

SOCRATES: We are. But not *only* in a book.

MACHIAVELLI: Oh.

SOCRATES: Do you really doubt whether you are real?

MACHIAVELLI: I do not want to investigate such metaphysical questions. My interest is elsewhere.

SOCRATES: So you are not even *interested* in whether you are real or not?

MACHIAVELLI: Socrates, you are a very annoying little man!

SOCRATES: Am I to interpret that as your answer to my question?

MACHIAVELLI: You are to interpret that as my *impatience* with your question. You led me to believe that we were going to investigate my *book*.

SOCRATES: My apologies. Since we have a virtually unlimited time in this world, the habit of impatience is quite pointless here. I have been here for many centuries and have adjusted; but you have just recently arrived and still carry old habits. I had forgotten that. My fault; please excuse me.

MACHIAVELLI: Your apology is a very clever insult, I think.

SOCRATES: Oh, dear; that's what they said about the longer, more famous *Apology* I made back in Athens, too!

MACHIAVELLI: Can we get back to *The Prince*, please?

SOCRATES: Of course. Let's see—we are considering your opinion about good and evil, or that for which men are praised and that for which they are condemned, as you call it.

Here is what you say in the chapter with that title, chapter 15. The chapter begins as follows:

Our next task is to consider the policies and principles a ruler ought to follow in dealing with his subjects or with his friends. Since I know many people have written on this subject, I am concerned it may be thought presumptuous for me to write on it as well, especially since what I have to say, as regards this question in particular, will differ greatly from the recommendations of others. But my

hope is to write a book that will be useful, at least to those who read it intelligently, and so I thought it sensible to go straight to a discussion of how things are in real life and not waste time with a discussion of an imaginary world. For many authors have constructed imaginary republics and principalities that have never existed in practice and never could; for the gap between how people actually behave and how they ought to behave is so great that anyone who ignores everyday reality in order to live up to an ideal will soon discover he has been taught how to destroy himself, not how to preserve himself. For anyone who wants to act the part of a good man in all circumstances will bring about his own ruin, for those he has to deal with will not all be good. So it is necessary for a ruler, if he wants to hold on to power, to learn how not to be good, and to know when it is and when it is not necessary to use this knowledge.

Wootton, p. 47, ll. 35–36; p. 48, ll. 1–18.

So the idealists taught men how to be good and perish; while you teach them how to be bad and succeed.

MACHIAVELLI: Exactly.

SOCRATES: Isn't it true that what is natural to us is naturally known?

MACHIAVELLI: Yes.

SOCRATES: And you say that man is bad by nature?

MACHIAVELLI: Yes.

SOCRATES: Then man knows by nature how to be bad.

MACHIAVELLI: That follows.

SOCRATES: But what is naturally known does not need to be taught.

MACHIAVELLI: I suppose that is so.

SOCRATES: So how to be bad does not need to be taught. We have always known how to be bad.

MACHIAVELLI: That follows.

SOCRATES: Then why do you teach it?

MACHIAVELLI: To teach princes to overcome scruples, which prevents them from being bad.

SOCRATES: So that they can use the knowledge they possess by nature?

MACHIAVELLI: Yes.

SOCRATES: Then you do not teach new knowledge, only a new unscrupulousness. You change men's wills, not their intellects. You are a kind of preacher rather than a teacher—an upside-down Savonarola, so to speak.

MACHIAVELLI: No, that is ridiculous! I give them facts, not sermons.

SOCRATES: Well, let us see what this claim of yours means. For it is your lasting legacy in political philosophy. After your death, most of the influential political philosophers for the next few centuries accepted the essential point you make in this passage, redefining politics as "the art of the possible", whereas all the philosophers before you defined it as part of *ethics*, the public or collective part.

MACHIAVELLI: Aha! So I *did* become the Columbus of political philosophy! So did the name "Machiavellian" become a part of the vocabulary of the whole human race, then?

SOCRATES: Well, yes, but not in the way you think.

MACHIAVELLI: But I thought you said I was credited with discovering a brave new world, like Columbus.

SOCRATES: Yes, but there remains the question of whether this world is habitable.

MACHIAVELLI: But you said my essential revolution was accepted by centuries of successors!

SOCRATES: Yes, but not without modification. Everyone saw the need to temper your radicalism somewhat. For instance, the Englishman Hobbes accepted your view of man as selfish, fear as his greatest passion, and war as his natural state, which he called "nasty, solitary, brutish, and short". But he added some notion of natural rights to this bleak picture. Even more popular was another Englishman named Locke, who accepted your notion that all men are avaricious, but thought that the new economic system based on free competition and capital—what you called usury or interest—could provide a non-moral substitute for moral virtue in making man prosperous and happy and peaceful. But he, too, added a notion of natural moral law.

MACHIAVELLI: Then they added mere postscripts, but I was the one who changed the text. Is this not so? Admit it, Socrates: I have displaced your famous pupil Plato, have I not? Isn't it true that because of me politics ceased to take its bearings by "the ideal" and instead, like a science, took its bearings from the real?

SOCRATES: Not completely.

MACHIAVELLI: Are there still political idealists?

SOCRATES: Yes, but not the way you think. The two most catastrophic political philosophies of the twentieth century, Marxism and Fascism, both began with a new "ideal" concept of socialized man that clashed so thoroughly with man's real nature that they both totally failed, after having murdered many, many millions in trying to achieve their goal.

MACHIAVELLI: Well, if anything justifies me, *that* does. Up with the real! Down with the ideal!

SOCRATES: That is what we must now investigate: your concept of the real and ideal.

12

Machiavelli's Metaphysics

MACHIAVELLI: I have *no* concept of the ideal. This is what I say to the ideal—Do you understand Italian hand language?

SOCRATES: It loses something in the translation to English, but it is not difficult to guess. For here is what you say about it in print. You contrast **"how things are in real life"** with **"an imaginary world"**; and with **"imaginary republics and principalities that have never existed"**.

MACHIAVELLI: That is correct.

SOCRATES: And when you refer to **"imaginary republics and principalities that have never existed"** you probably have in mind Plato's *Republic* first of all, is that correct?

MACHIAVELLI: Yes.

SOCRATES: So when we think of the "Platonic Forms" or "Platonic Ideas", especially Justice, which Plato tried to define in the *Republic*, we should keep in mind your contrast of "the real" with "the ideal" and call them "ideal", *not* "real"?

MACHIAVELLI: Yes.

SOCRATES: And the visible world, which Plato symbolized by the shadows in a cave, would be to you "the real"?

MACHIAVELLI: Yes. And if I wrote of such things, I would not use the symbol of shadows in a cave for this real world. I would use *that* symbol for Plato's ideas or ideals. They exist only in the cave of his imagination. Plato had the whole world inside out. His "images in the cave" are the real world, and his so-called real world outside the cave is only in his imagination.

SOCRATES: So "the real" or "the real truth" is what we see and how men actually live and what they do. And "the ideal" is what we imagine or think but do not see?

MACHIAVELLI: Yes, exactly.

SOCRATES: So "the real" is only what we can see?

MACHIAVELLI: Yes. What *someone* could see.

SOCRATES: What we can see always has color and shape, does it not?

MACHIAVELLI: I suppose so.

SOCRATES: And do goodness and evil have any color? Is the good perhaps green and evil red? Or do they have shape? Is goodness square and evil round?

MACHIAVELLI: Of course not. How silly!

SOCRATES: Then the real does not include good and evil.

MACHIAVELLI: That is the conclusion I draw. Good and evil are in our imagining or thinking or willing or feeling, not in the real world.

SOCRATES: So "there is nothing good or bad, but thinking makes it so."

MACHIAVELLI: A wise saying. I wish I had thought of it first. More precisely, it is not so much *thinking* as *willing*, and above all the power to enforce one's will. *That* is what makes good or evil. For whoever is able to make the laws defines good and evil by those laws. This is why I rank arms before laws in importance: because the cause is more important than the effect.

SOCRATES: So a cruel tyrant who commands unjust tortures and killings of innocent men is evil if another has the power to make laws declaring his deeds evil; but he is good if he has the power to make the laws according to his own will, laws that declare his injustices to be just and the innocent to be guilty.

MACHIAVELLI: That sounds shocking, but it is true. The rules are written by the winners. Rules are artificial, not real.

SOCRATES: The *moral* rules, you mean, not the *practical* rules for success. You put this latter kind of rule in "the real" when you explain why some evil tyrants like Agathocles flourish while others fail.

MACHIAVELLI: That is correct.

SOCRATES: Let me quote from chapter 8, **"Concerning Those Who Become Princes by Evil Means"**. Here is your wisdom about the real natural laws of success:

Some may wonder how it happened that Aga-thocles and others like him could so long re-main secure in their dominions after their countless acts of cruelty and treachery, and could defend themselves from foreign foes without ever being conspired against by the citizenry, while other men who also resorted to cruelty were unable to keep their states even in times of peace, not to mention the more uncertain times of war. I believe this is explained by proper and improper use of cruelty. It can be said to be properly used (if one may speak favorably of what is bad) when one resorts to it at one stroke out of a need for safety and does not thereafter insist upon it. . . . It is improperly used when, though rarely applied at the start, it is resorted to with increasing rather than decreasing fre-quency as time goes by. . . . Injuries must be committed all at once so that, being savored less, they will arouse less resentment. Bene-fits, on the other hand, should be bestowed little by little so as to be more fully savored.

Donno, p. 38, ll. 3–18, 33–36.

MACHIAVELLI: Now if that's not practical wisdom, I don't know what is.

SOCRATES: Oh, I don't doubt that it is just that.

MACHIAVELLI: And it doesn't *claim* to be moral wis-dom.

SOCRATES: No.

MACHIAVELLI: So what could be unwise in it?

SOCRATES: Perhaps it's not realistic after all.

MACHIAVELLI: You said you didn't doubt that.

SOCRATES: I said I didn't doubt it was *practical*. "Practical" means "it works when you practice it." Realistic means "true to reality".

MACHIAVELLI: And in the real world my advice works. I don't preach; I don't tell people whether to do the moral good or the moral evil. All I do is to tell them that as a matter of fact, in the real world a little evil often works better, and how, and why. I'm totally true to reality.

SOCRATES: This is true only if we grant your most fundamental assumption.

MACHIAVELLI: I make no assumptions. (That is one of the many ways you can distinguish me from the Virgin Mary.)

SOCRATES: You do, and you must. In fact, your assumption is a metaphysical assumption.

MACHIAVELLI: I eschew all metaphysics!

SOCRATES: You want to, but you do not and cannot. For in the argument you have just given, you have assumed that "reality" equals only the world we can see. That is a metaphysical assumption, an assumption about what reality is.

MACHIAVELLI: That is *not* a metaphysical assumption.

SOCRATES: Is it proved? Or do you offer arguments for it?

MACHIAVELLI: No—

SOCRATES: Then it is an assumption.

MACHIAVELLI: But it is not a *metaphysical* assumption. Damn it, Socrates, I'm a political scientist, not a metaphysician. I'm *anti*-metaphysics.

SOCRATES: What is metaphysics?

MACHIAVELLI: Flying beyond reality in our thoughts.

SOCRATES: Again you make a metaphysical assumption about how far "reality" extends. *You* mean by "reality" the visible world, do you not?

MACHIAVELLI: Yes.

SOCRATES: But others do not. They say reality includes moral ideals, values, laws, or goods.

MACHIAVELLI: And they are wrong. These things are subjective, not objective, as the idealists believe.

SOCRATES: Perhaps so. Perhaps not. But in either case the issue is one of metaphysics. For metaphysics is simply the study of what "reality" means. Now you and these "idealists" differ about that. Therefore your dispute is about metaphysics.

MACHIAVELLI: Hmph!

SOCRATES: Is there an argument hidden in that syllable somewhere?

MACHIAVELLI: I'm not arguing. I'm sulking.

SOCRATES: Could you translate your sulk into something like an argument?

MACHIAVELLI: You promised to examine my book!

SOCRATES: I thought that was what I was doing. Wasn't *The Prince* your book? Was it plagiarized?

MACHIAVELLI: I wrote a book about practical politics, and you cross-examine me on metaphysics. I claim only to heal the body politic, not to define it. Damn it, Socrates, I'm a physician, not a metaphysician!

SOCRATES: I thought I had just shown you that you do make metaphysical assumptions and what they are.

MACHIAVELLI: Why do you impose your metaphysical agenda on my political agenda? That is as unfair as my looking for political assumptions in your metaphysical arguments about being and becoming.

SOCRATES: I impose nothing; I only expose. It is the task of the philosopher to find and expose and examine assumptions.

MACHIAVELLI: But I am a political scientist!

SOCRATES: So?

MACHIAVELLI: Scientists don't assume anything; philosophers do.

SOCRATES: Not so. In fact, it is the opposite: it is philosophy that questions the assumptions of science, not science that questions the assumptions of philosophy.

MACHIAVELLI: Just because you found one so-called metaphysical assumption, that does not prove your general principle. Perhaps everyone has to make *one* metaphysical assumption. Can we move from the one to the many, from the exception to the rule? My book is full of practical politics, it is not full of metaphysics.

SOCRATES: Oh, but it is! For instance, here is another metaphysical assumption that you make. It comes in the passage where you criticize the traditional value of generosity, a moral value praised highly by both pagan and Christian, for instance by Aristotle in the *Nicomachean Ethics* and by Jesus in the Gospels. You say:

> **There is nothing so self-defeating as gen-erosity, for the more generous you are, the less you are able to be generous. Generosity leads to poverty and disgrace, or, if you try to escape that, to rapacity and hostility.**

Wootton, p. 50, ll. 34–38.

MACHIAVELLI: There is no assumption there and cer-tainly no metaphysics. It is a simple observation that if I have a thousand gold pieces and out of generos-ity give all of them away to make others rich, I have then lost the ability to be generous because I have no more gold to be generous with. And the same thing applies to power, arms, land, and even fame and glory. What is shared is diminished as far as my possession and control of it are concerned. The point is obvious: The more generous you are, the less generous you can be.

SOCRATES: That is true of material goods. They di-minish when shared. But does wisdom, love, trust, af-fection, beauty, or knowledge diminish when shared? Does a teacher become ignorant when he shares his knowledge with his students?

MACHIAVELLI: No . . .

SOCRATES: So you are assuming that only material things are real or good or important. And that is the metaphysical assumption of materialism.

MACHIAVELLI: That is not my metaphysics; it is only my scientific method. Science cannot *know* the invisible.

SOCRATES: It is your epistemology, then, your answer to the question: How do we *know* what is real?

MACHIAVELLI: Let it be my epistemology, then. Anything but metaphysics!

SOCRATES: Then we must look at this next.

13

Machiavelli's Epistemology

SOCRATES: In chapter 15 of *The Prince*, you contrasted **"how things are in real life"** with **"an imaginary world"**. So you equate a thing like Plato's *Republic* with "the imaginary"?

MACHIAVELLI: Yes, that's exactly what I had in mind.

SOCRATES: Let us see exactly what you have in your mind. Do you think we can imagine a tree?

MACHIAVELLI: Of course.

SOCRATES: Because we have first seen it, or because it is something innate in the mind?

MACHIAVELLI: What do you mean?

SOCRATES: If we had never seen a tree, would we be able to imagine one?

MACHIAVELLI: No.

SOCRATES: Then we can imagine only what we have seen.

MACHIAVELLI: Yes. Sensation is where the images come from.

SOCRATES: Can you also imagine a golden tree, a tree made of gold?

MACHIAVELLI: Yes.

SOCRATES: Is this because you have perceived both trees and gold with your senses and, then, combined them in your imagination?

MACHIAVELLI: Yes.

SOCRATES: So we can distinguish *three* acts here: sensing, imagining what we have sensed, and imagining something we have not sensed by rearranging the elements we have sensed.

MACHIAVELLI: Yes, that is clear. Why are we doing this abstract philosophizing about epistemology, or theory of knowledge? It is almost as abstract as metaphysics. Why not just look at what I wrote?

SOCRATES: Because you make epistemological assumptions in what you write, just as you make metaphysical assumptions in what you write.

MACHIAVELLI: Hmph!

SOCRATES: Now stop sulking and tell me this: Must all the things we imagine have sensible qualities like color and shape?

MACHIAVELLI: Yes.

SOCRATES: And do the following things has color and shape? Truth, goodness, justice, number, musical notes, the mind, feelings, the act of the will, and the mental energy by which you imagine a golden tree?

MACHIAVELLI: None of those abstract concepts have color or shape.

SOCRATES: Then it follows that they cannot be imagined.

MACHIAVELLI: Yes.

SOCRATES: But they can be known?

MACHIAVELLI: I am skeptical of that. Is that real knowledge or just playing with concepts?

SOCRATES: You told me that you know that these things have no color or shape, did you not?

MACHIAVELLI: Yes.

SOCRATES: Does a quasar have color or shape?

MACHIAVELLI: I have no idea. What is a quasar?

SOCRATES: You do not know what quasars are. And therefore you do not know anything about their attributes, such as color or shape. But you do know what these other nine things that I listed are, for you know that their nature prevents them from having color or shape.

MACHIAVELLI: All right, I do know that much.

SOCRATES: So you know these things—justice, for instance—even though they have no color or shape and therefore cannot be sensed or imagined.

MACHIAVELLI: I suppose so.

SOCRATES: And when you say that **"many authors have constructed imaginary republics and principalities that have never existed in practice and never could,"** you have in mind a book like Plato's *Republic*, a book that attempts to define Justice—perfect justice, ideal justice.

MACHIAVELLI: Yes.

SOCRATES: Which has never existed and thus never been seen.

MACHIAVELLI: Right.

SOCRATES: If it has never been seen, how can it be imagined?

MACHIAVELLI: It can't.

SOCRATES: Yet you call such a book "imaginary".

MACHIAVELLI: I simply meant "unreal". It is not even "imaginary" in your precise sense of that term as we have just defined it. Justice has no color or shape, so it cannot be imagined.

SOCRATES: But you say it has **"never have existed in practice and never could"**. Surely it has been known, though not seen. Many have written about justice, and surely some have written some truth— you yourself, for instance.

MACHIAVELLI: That is not real knowledge. That is just speculation.

SOCRATES: So you say all "real knowledge" comes from sense experience?

MACHIAVELLI: Yes.

SOCRATES: And is limited to sense experience and what we can imagine from it?

MACHIAVELLI: Yes.

SOCRATES: You are what later philosophers will call an empiricist.

MACHIAVELLI: Fine. Sticks and stones may break my bones, but names will never hurt me.

SOCRATES: How, then, can you speak of justice or of good and evil or any such things if you do not believe that in addition to the outer eye of the sense there is the inner eye of reason?

MACHIAVELLI: Oh, I do not deny reason.

SOCRATES: What do you say it is?

MACHIAVELLI: It is the power of calculating, inductively or deductively. But all that it calculates comes from the senses.

SOCRATES: So reason is the servant or scout of the senses?

MACHIAVELLI: Yes.

SOCRATES: Is it not vice versa? Isn't reason like a king who sends out his servants, the senses, to scout his kingdom and bring back information for the king to judge?

MACHIAVELLI: In philosophy, perhaps, but not in science. In science the data judge the theory. The ideas do not judge the sense data, but vice versa. My book is science—historical and political science.

SOCRATES: I see. So that is why you often contrast these two things—ideas and sense data—and always rank sense experience before ideas?

MACHIAVELLI: Yes.

SOCRATES: For instance, at the beginning of your chapter justifying lying and betraying friends, promises, and treaties—the one entitled **"How Far Rulers Are to Keep Their Word"**—chapter 18 it is—you set up an opposition between knowledge and sense experience. You write:

> **Everybody recognizes how praiseworthy it is for a ruler to keep his word and to live a life of integrity, without relying on craftiness. Nevertheless, we see that in practice, in these days, those rulers who have not thought it important to keep their word have achieved great things. . . . In the end, they have been able to overcome those who have placed store in integrity.**

Wootton, p. 53, ll. 29–32, 34–35.

MACHIAVELLI: Oh, I know how you will criticize that, Socrates. You will say that the martyr has really overcome his slayer, and the poor saint has overcome the rich sinner, and the honest citizen has overcome the ruler who deceives and enslaves him, because you are concerned with success in the next world rather than in this one, just like Plato.

SOCRATES: Actually Plato tried to prove in the *Republic* that "justice is always more profitable than injustice" *in this world*, even if there were no next world.

MACHIAVELLI: Well, then, it is virtue you and Plato are concerned with rather than happiness and success and profit.

SOCRATES: Actually, "happiness" is what Plato was most concerned with. He claimed to prove that virtue —especially justice—was the cause of happiness; that "justice is always more profitable than injustice."

MACHIAVELLI: Well, then, it is the soul rather than the body that you are concerned with.

SOCRATES: Well, of course! Aren't you too? Is that not where all happiness, and all consciousness of success, lies? Is it your fingernails that are happy? Can a corpse be happy? But I do not want to press that point now. It is your epistemology we are after. Though it is very easy to become diverted and to chase another quarry instead, for all the animals are interdependent in this jungle: your anthropology, your metaphysics, your ethics, and your epistemology. We cannot separate these animals from each other if we let them run free. We can separate them only if we put them in our artificial cages. This is why my investigation of your practical politics cannot avoid investigating all these other aspects of your philosophy.

In fact, the very next thing you bring up in the passage I was reading is—once again—an anthropology, a philosophy of man. (We never really left this subject, you know, when we investigated your metaphysics or your ethics or your epistemology.)

Here is your next point, a memorable one for all readers:

> [T]here are two ways to fight: one while respecting the rules, the other with no holds barred. Men alone fight in the first fashion, and animals fight in the second. But because you cannot always win if you respect the rules, you must be prepared to break them. A ruler, in particular, needs to know how to be both an animal and a man.
> . . . So you see a wise ruler cannot, and should not, keep his word when doing so is to his disadvantage. . . . Of course, if all

Wootton, p.
54, ll. 1–5,
20–21, 23–25.

**men were good, this advice would be bad;
but since men are wicked and will not keep
faith with you, you need not keep faith with
them.**

MACHIAVELLI: Remember, Socrates, I am speaking
here of the *practical* "ought". My point is simply that
sometimes promises must be broken in order to succeed. Sometimes even in order to survive.

SOCRATES: Let me see whether I understand your
reasoning here. For instance, do you mean that a
second-century Christian who promised never to
commit idolatry, when given the choice by the Roman emperor to worship the emperor as a god or to
be fed to the lions in the coliseum, ought to break
his promise?

MACHIAVELLI: Well, of course. That is a very clear
case of the practical ought conflicting with the moral
ought. But I was concerned with promises made to
men, not to God. That is why the last sentence you
read is my justification.

SOCRATES [reading]: **"[I]f all men were good, this
advice would be bad."**

MACHIAVELLI: That is because if all men were good,
there would never be the need to make the choice between martyrdom or idolatry. But that situation exists
only in the ideal world, not the real world.

SOCRATES [reading]: **"But since men are wicked
and will not keep faith with you, you need not
keep faith with them."**

MACHIAVELLI: There! I have said it. I'm sure this shocks you, Socrates. Will you refute it with a sermon or with a subtle metaphysical argument?

SOCRATES: Neither; with a sense observation.

MACHIAVELLI: No way! That's *my* chosen battlefield.

SOCRATES: You say that all **"men are wicked and will not keep faith with you."** But surely, some men *do* keep promises.

MACHIAVELLI: A few. But many more break them.

SOCRATES: Does your precept depend on whether there are more promise-breakers than promise-keepers?

MACHIAVELLI: It depends, not on the objective fact that there *are* a certain number of both, but on the subjective fact that you never know with certainty whether the man you are dealing with is going to keep his promises or break them.

SOCRATES: Then *that* is your assumption: that you never know this.

MACHIAVELLI: Yes.

SOCRATES: I would question that assumption because of its inadequate epistemology.

MACHIAVELLI: What?! What's your quarrel with my epistemology?

SOCRATES: You are an empiricist. I agree that you can never know a man's character by mere sense observation. But surely there are other ways of knowing a man's character.

MACHIAVELLI: None that I know.

SOCRATES: Oh, my. Then you will certainly never be a successful prince.

MACHIAVELLI: You seem to equate "successful" with "naïve".

SOCRATES: Not at all. I would equate "successful" with "realistic".

MACHIAVELLI: So would I.

SOCRATES: And I would equate "realistic" with "knowing what is real and acting accordingly".

MACHIAVELLI: So would I, though I would not include any ideal society over and above the real one in my definition of what is real.

SOCRATES: But do you know the one you call real? Do you know that no society can hold together without promises? (I mean making them and keeping them and trusting others to keep them.) What society has ever worked by mistrust? For society must bind man to men, and present to future, and how can that be done without promise-keeping?

MACHIAVELLI: Oh, I know all that, Socrates.

SOCRATES: Then why do you give advice that, if it is believed and obeyed, will surely destroy society instead of preserving it? And how can you call this advice "practical"?

MACHIAVELLI: Because my book was not written for a whole society, like Plato's *Republic*—*res publica*, "public things"—but for a single prince. As you yourself pointed out when contrasting our two titles, *The Prince* was not written for public consumption.

SOCRATES: So for it to work, the citizens must believe lies and the prince alone know the truth about no one being trustworthy?

MACHIAVELLI: Something like that, certainly. If the sheep were foxes, the shepherd could not keep them orderly and happy. Nor could the shepherd do that if he were a sheep.

SOCRATES: And you call this a single society even though the shepherd and the sheep, the prince and the people, have such opposite philosophies?

MACHIAVELLI: If the dark and esoteric wisdom were not known to the prince, he would not be able to be a successful prince. And if the simple and exoteric naïveté were not believed by the people, they would not trust each other or the prince.

SOCRATES: Your prince seems almost of another species—as superior to his people in wisdom as a fox, or a shepherd, is to his sheep.

MACHIAVELLI: Just like Plato's philosopher-king! Although the esoteric wisdom of Platonic philosophy is almost exactly the opposite of mine, both of us see the need for this sharp difference between ruler and people. I sense that you do not agree.

SOCRATES: I do not.

MACHIAVELLI: Because you are naïve and optimistic about mankind.

SOCRATES: No, because I am *not*. I believe that power tends to corrupt. I saw a very corrupt democracy in my lifetime and also a very corrupt oligarchy and many very corrupt tyrannies.

MACHIAVELLI: But you were killed by a democracy, not by a prince.

SOCRATES: True.

MACHIAVELLI: So you must agree with Plato that democracy is one of the worst forms of government.

SOCRATES: No, I do not.

MACHIAVELLI: Because you have such faith in mankind that you want to give the power to rule into the hands of all, even the sheep!

SOCRATES: No, because I have such little faith in mankind that I do not want to give such power to rule into the hands of any prince.

MACHIAVELLI: Oh, well, I admire your premise but not your conclusion.

SOCRATES: My fear is that your prince will think of himself as a god.

MACHIAVELLI: He is somewhat godlike. But a god can serve his people, and even suffer for them, especially if he is raised with Christian principles.

SOCRATES: Some time soon I would like you to read a little fantasy written a few centuries after your death about such a prince. It is called "The Grand Inquisitor". In it, the author (a man named Dostoyevsky) imagines Christ come back to earth in Spain and arrested by the Inquisition—

MACHIAVELLI: Oh, ho! What a brilliant satirical plot!

SOCRATES: The Inquisitor argues with him, claiming that he, Torquemada, is really the more Christian prince, the more compassionate one, since he keeps the sheep docile and happy, while Christ makes them unhappy with the burden of conscience and free choice.

MACHIAVELLI: You know, he has a point there—

SOCRATES: I suspected you would say that. Your prince sounds disturbingly like the Grand Inquisitor.

MACHIAVELLI: But to come back from fantasy to reality, I prove that it is necessary for the prince to be a fox and not always keep promises, since other princes do not keep theirs. I write:

> **Nor is a ruler ever short of legitimate reasons to justify breaking his word. I could give an infinite number of contemporary examples to support my argument and to show how treaties and promises have been rendered null and void by the dishonesty of rulers; and he who has known best how to act the fox has come out of it the best. But it is essential to know how to conceal how crafty one is, to know how to be a clever counterfeit and hypocrite.**

Wootton, p. 54, ll. 25–31.

SOCRATES: There will be a popular song about that a few centuries after your time: "The Great Pretender".

MACHIAVELLI: So my wisdom was recognized by all the populace through this song?

SOCRATES: Well, no. The song wasn't *that* popular.

MACHIAVELLI: Was it about successful politics?

SOCRATES: No, about unsuccessful love.

MACHIAVELLI: But my advice *did* become famous?

SOCRATES: "Infamous" would be a more exact word. For your own exact word for your "pretender" is the word "hypocrite". At least that was the term used by the most influential teacher of all time.

MACHIAVELLI: Far be it from me to contradict him, especially here—and especially when claiming to teach what is practical!

SOCRATES: So you claim *not* to contradict him?

MACHIAVELLI: I think his teachings coincide with mine in many places. For instance, he advised us to "be wise as serpents and innocent as doves" (Mt 10:16). It is also written that "many believed in his name when they saw the signs which he did; but Jesus did not trust himself to them, because he knew all men and needed no one to bear witness of man; for he himself knew what was in man" (Jn 2:23–25).

SOCRATES: Granted that many of his followers have neglected to be wise as serpents in their eagerness to be innocent as doves, do you claim that you do not neglect to be dovelike in your eagerness to be serpentine?

MACHIAVELLI: *Someone* has to redress the balance! Both Christ and Christians are often thought to be naïve simpletons.

SOCRATES: You have a point.

MACHIAVELLI: In fact, I think I have learned much from him, even in this notorious chapter in which I speak of the need for lying.

SOCRATES: And what could that possibly be?

MACHIAVELLI: How did he ensure that his kingdom (which, of course, was "not of this world") would continue for many centuries to sway minds and wills and hearts? By propaganda. He was the first to understand its power. And I was the second.

SOCRATES: I would hardly feel comfortable using *that* term to describe—

MACHIAVELLI: No, you wouldn't. You are only a dove and not a serpent.

SOCRATES: He didn't say "be as *deceitful* as serpents"!

MACHIAVELLI: Socrates, I *must* know how successful my understanding of propaganda proved to be after my death. Please tell me, were there great princes after me who used this weapon to great effect?

SOCRATES: Oh, yes. There was one named Adolf Hitler, who won his nation's passionate devotion by propaganda and almost conquered the world.

MACHIAVELLI: Now there is my vindication!

SOCRATES: I—um—would not advise you to claim him as your disciple.

MACHIAVELLI: Why not?

SOCRATES: Because after his death he was hated more than any other man in history.

MACHIAVELLI: Oh. Then his propaganda was not adequate.

SOCRATES: There were some other problems—

MACHIAVELLI: But my vindication is here, in my book, which we have been neglecting. Can we get back to it and to our appointed task?

SOCRATES: Yes, surely. Please forgive my distractability and absent-mindedness. It seems to be a professional hazard among philosophers.

MACHIAVELLI: So here are my conclusions:

Wootton, p.   **So a ruler need not have all the positive qual-**
55, ll. 5–6.   **ities . . . but he must seem to have them.**

SOCRATES: So appearance is more important than reality?

MACHIAVELLI: Exactly. Image is everything.

SOCRATES: That became a slogan for success in advertising five centuries after you.

MACHIAVELLI: See? I told you so. What is "advertising"?

SOCRATES: Essentially, propaganda.

MACHIAVELLI: Again, I told you so.

SOCRATES: It is the world's oldest profession. It was invented by a serpent in a garden.

MACHIAVELLI: **"Indeed, I would go so far as to say that if you have them** [positive qualities] **and never make any exceptions, then you will suffer for it;**

while if you merely appear to have them, they will benefit you."

Wootton, p. 55, ll. 6–9.

SOCRATES: Plato and all the classical moralists tried to prove exactly the opposite: that justice is always profitable, that virtue works, that right makes might.

MACHIAVELLI: And they had it completely backward!

SOCRATES: They gave reasons for their conclusion.

MACHIAVELLI: And so do I!

SOCRATES: I think you can guess my next question.

MACHIAVELLI: Here is my reason for preferring the control of appearance to the control of reality:

[M]en judge by the eye rather than the hand, for all men can see a thing, but few come close enough to touch it. All men see what you seem to be; only a few will know what you are.

Donno, p. 63, ll. 40–42, p. 64, l. 1.

SOCRATES: So you prefer appearance to reality.

MACHIAVELLI: Of course. As your advertiser said: "Image is everything."

SOCRATES: And truth is nothing.

MACHIAVELLI: Comparatively.

SOCRATES: Is that really true?

MACHIAVELLI: I believe it is.

SOCRATES: But truth is nothing. So that is really nothing.

MACHIAVELLI: Your argument is a mere sophism, Socrates; that is unworthy of you.

SOCRATES: No, Niccolò, your saying is a logical self-contradiction that is unworthy of you.

MACHIAVELLI: Are we in a logic class now or in the real world?

SOCRATES: I know of nothing more universally true and practical in the real world than the laws of logic. Do you? Have you ever seen anything that did not obey the law of non-contradiction? For instance, a man who both existed and did not exist at the same time?

MACHIAVELLI: No.

SOCRATES: Then I think it is time to turn more explicitly to your logic.

14

Machiavelli's Logic

MACHIAVELLI: You have already found one self-contradiction in my book by your logical standards, and I'm sure you will find more. But I do not care: logic is the most abstract of all studies, so it is the least important to me. I am a practical man, remember?

SOCRATES: But because you are a practical man, you should take logic more seriously. For to be practical is to know how to deal with what is real; and to know how to deal with what is real, you must know what is real; and logic is the science of everything that is real or even imaginary. Its laws are obeyed by not just some things but all. Therefore the first requirement for anyone who would be practical is to know logic.

MACHIAVELLI: Go ahead, then, Socrates, play your logic games.

SOCRATES: Oh, they are neither games nor mine, for both games and what is mine are changeable.

MACHIAVELLI: Fine. Get it over with. Whatever.

SOCRATES: We have already found one self-contradiction: your prioritizing appearance over reality and truth.

MACHIAVELLI: That is *not* a self-contradiction. I do not prefer a knowledge of appearances to a knowledge of reality for myself, or for my prince whom I am advising, but for the people he rules over.

SOCRATES: Ah, so you *are* concerned with being logical. You would not, then, agree with the poet Walt Whitman—another man centuries after you—who said, "Do I contradict myself? Very well, then, I contradict myself. I am large; I contain multitudes."

MACHIAVELLI: Of course not. This man might be a poet but never a prince.

SOCRATES: You are right. Let me grant, then, that your preference for appearance over reality for the people is not a logical contradiction, only a justification of dishonesty and hypocrisy. Here is a second case, which we have already seen: your argument about good arms and good laws.

MACHIAVELLI: That is not a self-contradiction either. It is only a *non sequitur*.

SOCRATES: Aha! You not only care about logic, you also know its rules. Yes, you are right: your argument contained, not a self-contradiction, but a logical fallacy, a *non sequitur*. Your conclusion does not logically follow from your premise. Even if good arms are a necessary cause of good laws (which they are not), it does not follow that they are a sufficient cause.

MACHIAVELLI: Anything else, Socrates?

SOCRATES: Another *non sequitur* which I believe we pointed out is the one where you say that if men were good, the precept to break promises would not hold, but since men are bad to you and break their promises, it follows that you are morally justified in breaking your promise to them.

MACHIAVELLI: Why is that a *non sequitur*?

SOCRATES: Hmm—perhaps it is not. Let us see. The premise is that men do in fact break their promises to you. The conclusion is that you are morally right to break your promises to them. The conclusion has in it something that is not in the premise: it is about what is morally right to do, while the premise is only about what is in fact done. So as it stands, the argument claims to prove *values* from *facts* alone. And that seems to be a *non sequitur*. However, if you add the implied but not expressed premise that it is morally right to do to others whatever they in fact do to you, the conclusion then logically follows.

MACHIAVELLI: So it is not a logical self-contradiction and not even a *non sequitur*. So far my logic seems to be standing up quite well.

SOCRATES: But without this premise, your argument is logically invalid. And the premise in question is pretty obviously false.

MACHIAVELLI: Is it? Why?

SOCRATES: Why, suppose others do to you what is morally wrong.

MACHIAVELLI: An easy supposition.

SOCRATES: According to your premise—that it is morally right to do to others whatever they do to you—it is then morally right for you to do to them the same moral wrongs they do to you.

MACHIAVELLI: Yes, I said that.

SOCRATES: So you are saying that it is morally right to do what is morally wrong. That wrong is right, evil is good. That is a self-contradiction.

MACHIAVELLI: Somehow that does not bother me much. I would rather fail logic and succeed in politics than fail in politics and succeed in logic. What other charges do you bring against me, O great logician?

SOCRATES: Only two more. One is very general, about your ideals, and one very specific, about your practical advice.

MACHIAVELLI: I care only about the specific, so let us get the general one out of the way first, and quickly.

SOCRATES: If we can. You are not in charge here, nor am I, but we both must follow the argument wherever it leads, like rafters on a river.

My question concerns the relation between the real and the ideal. What is your most basic criticism of the political philosophies taught before your day, both pagan and Christian? Why do you reject their common principle that we must judge what we see by ideals or that the goal of the state is virtue in all its citizens?

MACHIAVELLI: The ideals of the ancients were very high and holy and beautiful, like the stars. But if we need to cross a dangerous mountain or canyon at night, they are too far away to be of much help. Much more light is shed on earthly things by a lantern, though its light and beauty are less than those of the stars. The nearness is greater, so the usefulness is greater.

SOCRATES: In other words, we should lower our ideals, and then they will become realizable.

MACHIAVELLI: Exactly. In practice, we need what is practical. And that is known by observation of men and what they have in fact done, not by the mystical musings of monks or the wordy abstractions of philosophers.

SOCRATES: So you judge ideals like those of Plato or Jesus to be too high to serve man as he is.

MACHIAVELLI: Yes. Man is an animal, not an angel; a sinner, not a saint.

SOCRATES: So you are judging the ideal by the actual.

MACHIAVELLI: Yes.

SOCRATES: And "the ideal" means the standard.

MACHIAVELLI: Yes.

SOCRATES: The standard for judging something.

MACHIAVELLI: Yes.

SOCRATES: Something actual.

MACHIAVELLI: Yes.

SOCRATES: So in judging the ideal by the actual, you are using that which *is to be judged* as the *judge* of that which is *to judge*. Is that not like a prisoner, accused of a crime, judging his judge and jury? Is this not something very near to a logical self-contradiction?

MACHIAVELLI: No. It is realism. The alternative to realistic and practically realizable ideals is unrealistic and unrealizable ideals—perfectionism.

SOCRATES: For instance, "Be ye perfect as your Father in Heaven is perfect"?

MACHIAVELLI: Well, yes. I have no wish to offend or speak against his teaching or his authority here, but I do not think he could have meant his counsels of perfection to be followed in the material world by sinful, fallen man.

SOCRATES: Then why do you think he said that?

MACHIAVELLI: I'm no theologian! How should I know?

SOCRATES: He was not speaking to theologians. Or monks or mystics.

MACHIAVELLI: Then I simply have no idea. Do you?

SOCRATES: Yes.

MACHIAVELLI: Well, excuse me! I have not been in this world long enough to be privy to the knowledge you have been given from above.

SOCRATES: No, it is not divine or other-worldly knowledge that tells me what he probably meant, but merely good sense and reason: How can a standard be less than perfect? If a runner does not aim at the finish line each moment, he will not make progress toward it; and if the student does not aim at the perfection of a perfect grade, he will wrongly judge an imperfect grade to be the ideal. In fact, unless we aim at and judge by an *eternal* standard, how can we ever judge that any temporal change is progress? If the goal line moves, how can the runner progress toward it? Do you see the point? It is simple logic.

MACHIAVELLI: Perhaps, then, I teach a new logic for a new ethics.

SOCRATES: What could you mean by that?

MACHIAVELLI: That sometimes moral evils are necessities and, thus, goods.

SOCRATES: So "Evil, be thou my good"? Even your *moral* good?

MACHIAVELLI: In a sense, yes. I shall have to remember that striking saying.

SOCRATES: It has already been used by a poet named Milton who put those words into the mouth of the Devil.

MACHIAVELLI: Of whom some call me the son. Well, that is not safe company to hobnob with, I think.

SOCRATES: Nor is it logically intelligible to call evil good. It is like calling up down or no yes. It is simply meaningless.

MACHIAVELLI: But it is meaningful if we distinguish the moral good from the practical good. Then, "evil, be thou my good" means simply that moral evil is accepted as practically good or useful to me. That's all I meant.

SOCRATES: So you would not claim that moral evil can sometimes be *morally* good?

MACHIAVELLI: No. That is a contradiction, as you pointed out. I do not teach morality, only practicality. I go beyond moral good and evil—say, there's a nice slogan, "beyond good and evil". I think I'd like to write a book by that title some time.

SOCRATES: It has been done by a man named Nietzsche. And his idea suffers the same logical fate: self-contradiction. For the idea is that it is *good* to go "beyond good and evil".

MACHIAVELLI: Well, then, let's try a third slogan for another idealism. How about this one:—"The end justifies the means."

SOCRATES: That is what people think you said.

MACHIAVELLI: Well, I never actually said it. But I wish I had. It's a catchy little slogan.

SOCRATES: And one that is obviously true in a sense, in fact trivially and tautologically true: *of course* the end for which a means is sought is the justification or reason for the means. That's what a "means" *means*: a means to an *end*. But that "justification" is only psychological: my desire for the end accounts for and causes my desire for the means. For instance, I desire a boat only because I desire to cross the sea.

But if when you say "the end justifies the means" you mean a *moral* justification—well, then, let us see. A *morally* good end justifies a *morally* good means. For instance, saving a man from starvation justifies giving him food. And a morally good end justifies a morally neutral means. For instance, building a cathedral justifies using a shovel. But does a morally good end justify a morally bad means? Would it be good to kill the rich if it served the end of better food for the poor?

MACHIAVELLI: Yes, under some circumstances it would. If it would contribute to the greatest good for the greatest number.

SOCRATES: You are now inventing another famous formula, the formula for the good, the goal or end or standard of moral judgment according to a philosophy that will be called utilitarianism. It bears strong resemblances to yours. Its formula is "the greatest happiness for the greatest number". That is the end that they say morally justifies any means that effectively attains it.

MACHIAVELLI: I was more concerned with the individual prince in my book than with "the greatest number", but I see nothing logically wrong with that moral principle. Do you?

SOCRATES: Yes. Suppose you were neither a sadist nor a masochist, and you were in a room with a hundred sadists. The greatest happiness for the greatest number of people in that room would be attained by means of those hundred sadists torturing you slowly and horribly to death. But would that be *morally good*?

MACHIAVELLI: No. Of course not. But I did not say that the end justified any means for all men in all of life. I did not write a book about ethics, remember? Nor is it about success for all, or even for one in private life or in business. I said, however, that in order for a prince to attain the end of princely success, which is power and empire, he must use means that are morally bad. He must therefore often choose between the practical good and the moral good. And is not this what Jesus himself said when he warned his disciples that they, too, would be persecuted and killed if they followed his moral way? Not only do I see no contradiction with logic, I do not even see any contradiction between what I say and what Jesus and the saints say. We present the same alternatives: either the moral or the practical.

SOCRATES: Then why did his disciples and yours make opposite choices between these two, the practical and the moral? If you are teaching the same lesson, then one of you is a very bad teacher.

15

Machiavelli's Life

SOCRATES: But I have one more seeming logical contradiction to ask you about. And I think it is the one you will take most seriously.

MACHIAVELLI: I am all ears.

SOCRATES: Your goal is the triumph of *virtù* over *fortuna*, or the conquest of fortune, is it not?

MACHIAVELLI: Yes.

SOCRATES: Philosophers shortly after you will call this "man's conquest of nature". They will declare this to be the end and purpose of man's life on earth, thus ushering in a whole new era with a new *summum bonum*, or greatest good.

MACHIAVELLI: I was truly a pioneer, then.

SOCRATES: Yes—although your version of this conquest was addressed, as you say, to the individual prince only; and to the conquest of other men more than to the conquest of nature; and by means of arms more than by technology.

Let us first see exactly what our data is before we evaluate it. In your penultimate chapter, you sum up and generalize all your practical advice. This is chapter 25, **"How Much Fortune Can Achieve in**

Human Affairs, and How It Is to Be Resisted". It is clearly your most important chapter.

MACHIAVELLI: I do not agree. If I had thought that, I would have put it last. For in practical things, the end is the most important, and it is attained last. In theoretical things, the *principle* is the most important, and it comes first. Therefore in books of philosophy the first chapter is usually the most important, but in books of systematic practical advice like mine, it is the last chapter.

You will note that the last chapter deals with something particular—the situation in Italy in my time—while the penultimate chapter deals with something general—the power of fortune. The practical is always particular.

It is also aimed at action, not thought, and is expressed in imperative sentences, while theory is aimed at mere thinking for its own sake and is expressed in indicative sentences. Thus my last chapter is an **"Exhortation to Seize Italy and Free Her from the Barbarians"**.

Frankly, Socrates, I am surprised that you did not understand this. I am surprised that it is I who am giving you this little lesson in some of the basics of the logic of Aristotle, your greatest student's greatest student, concerning the difference between theoretical and practical science.

SOCRATES: Thank you for the reminder, Niccolò. Indeed, I know all of these things, but *my* interest here is not primarily Italy or barbarians (by which you meant Frenchmen!) but timeless truths and your immortal soul and mind. As I told you, we do not read the *Times* here; we read the eternities.

Also, I did not want to believe that you invented this whole great machine, this whole radically new world view and life view, just to get the barbarians out of Italy. It is like inventing a bomb to crush a mouse.

MACHIAVELLI: That was not my first purpose in writing *The Prince*. As you pointed out in the beginning, it was a job application. I was trying to sell Lorenzo my intellectual *virtù* for some of his political *fortuna*.

SOCRATES: And if it had succeeded, it would have produced still another logical contradiction, or rather a practical contradiction, which I'm sure is much more distressing to you.

MACHIAVELLI: How's that again? I must have missed a few steps in your argument there.

SOCRATES: Suppose you had succeeded in convincing Lorenzo to employ you and your advice in this book. One piece of your advice is not to trust your subordinates. You also say that the ruler must not appear to be receiving advice from others but should claim all his wisdom as his own. If you had succeeded in persuading Lorenzo to take your advice, the human race would be reading, not *The Prince* by Niccolò Machiavelli, but *The Prince* by Lorenzo de' Medici. The book would have brought about your failure.

MACHIAVELLI: No, for my book was not the weapon by which I would triumph but only the Trojan horse to get within his walls. It was a mere pawn move on the chessboard. I would have used other pieces, other moves, other strategies that I do not reveal in this book if Lorenzo had taken my bait.

SOCRATES: Knowing *that* makes it difficult to take your book seriously. So its aim is not to reveal objective and universal truth, which is the aim of any science, but only to deceive one man and attain personal power?

MACHIAVELLI: No, not *only* that. As a means to that personal end, I revealed much true and scientific knowledge. Even if you cannot share my end, you can still share my means.

SOCRATES: Yes, but it makes it difficult to trust what you said when we know why you said it.

MACHIAVELLI: That need not be so. Suppose you found out that Euclid had written his *Geometry* only to deceive a prospective patron into showering him with riches; would that discovery make Euclid's geometrical principles untrue?

SOCRATES: No. You are right there. And that is why my investigation of your book has been philosophical rather than practical; because philosophy's end is universal truth, while the end of an individual's practice is some individual gain.

So let us return to our objective data, your book —although it might be illuminating also later to return to the consideration of your motives, your life, and your successes and failures insofar as they cast a light on your book. But I wish to save that for last so that we do not commit the fallacy you rightly warn us against: judging that a thinker's ideas are false or useless simply because you judge his motives or life or personality to be defective. This fallacy became very common a few centuries after your death, largely due to a man named Freud, who discovered many of the hidden mechanisms of the psyche and of motivation. (I shall examine one of his books some time, too.) The fallacy has been called "the psychological fallacy" or "the genetic fallacy", a version of the old fallacy of *ad hominem*.

So let us turn to your concluding judgments concerning fortune.

MACHIAVELLI: Thank you for being so fair, Socrates. I suppose you don't get to where you are in this place in any other way, do you? Or *do* you?

SOCRATES: No. Don't even think about it. Let us instead focus on your words—

MACHIAVELLI: How many times are you going to say "let us do it" before you *do* it?

SOCRATES: You shame me into action. You see, I was never a prince, and the one time I was compelled to enter the public and political arena, I could not even save my own life and my honor and honesty at the same time. You know the story, I'm sure, having read my *Apology*.

MACHIAVELLI: If you had had the opportunity to read my book in your lifetime, you would not have those regrets. See, this is why you need me even now—

SOCRATES: No. I have no regrets and no need for you. It is you who have need for me.

MACHIAVELLI: I think we have just proved, in the laboratory of life, that you also need me to give you a verbal kick in the posterior, or else you will keep *saying* "let us do it" and never do it. Only the combination of the man of thought and the man of action can be complete and completely successful, whether at thought or in action. I am the man of action; you are the man of thought. I am the lion; you are the fox.

SOCRATES: You presented yourself to Lorenzo with the same argument, but there you said *you* were the fox. Again you contradict yourself. *He* did not employ you; why should I?

MACHIAVELLI: Because I have already shown you my power in diverting you many times from your intended plan. And I could have done so many times more if I had not now confessed to you my strategy.

SOCRATES: Since we have been sailing so close to the wind of the psychological fallacy, I will *not* defer this topic of investigating your life and the light it may shed on your book, but I will pursue it now and defer my logical critique of the practical advice in your last chapter until the end. For I am the rower of our boat, not you, though the river's power and direction are from another, or what you call *fortuna*.

MACHIAVELLI: You would never make a good writer of fiction, either. Your image is internally inconsistent: your "boat" is both sailboat and rowboat.

SOCRATES: That is why I did not attempt to write fiction—or anything else, either, by the way. But what is at issue here is your writings, not mine.

I began this whole investigation by exposing the fundamental assumption of your philosophy of man, the hidden premise necessary for many of your conclusions. We found ourselves returning to this premise again and again, for we found you sailing forth from the home port of this premise again and again. I shall now quote your most explicit statement of this premise, which is not from *The Prince* but from your *Discourses*; and then I shall reveal the reasons, in your experience rather than in your argument, that seem to have led you to it.

MACHIAVELLI: But you said—

SOCRATES: No, I will not be distracted again. The principle reads:

It is necessary for anyone establishing a state and setting down its laws to presuppose that all men are evil, and that they will always act according to the wickedness of their spirits whenever they get the chance.

Discourses, book 1, chap. 3.

MACHIAVELLI: You said that many of my successors accepted this realistic view but tempered it a bit—

SOCRATES: At least one of your influential admirers, who was himself a prince as well as something of a philosopher, modified you in the opposite direction. He wrote an introduction to *The Prince* in which he said that "Machiavelli did not have enough contempt for humanity."

MACHIAVELLI: What a profound critique! Tell me more about this man.

SOCRATES: He wrote, "Machiavelli was the greatest Italian philosopher—"

MACHIAVELLI: Ha! Ha! Take *that*, Thomas Aquinas!

SOCRATES: "—the teacher of all teachers of politics."

MACHIAVELLI: You say that this wise man was a prince and a philosopher.

SOCRATES: Yes. I did not say he was a wise man, however.

MACHIAVELLI: What did he do? Where did he rule?

SOCRATES: He ruled Italy—

MACHIAVELLI: All Italy?

SOCRATES: Yes. As dictator, "Il Duce".

MACHIAVELLI: What were his aims?

SOCRATES: He sought to restore the ancient greatness of the Rome of the Caesars. The ancient Romans were his models, as they were yours.

MACHIAVELLI: *Mirabile dictu!*

SOCRATES: Actually this man did perform a great miracle that was visible to all Italians: he made the trains run on time.

MACHIAVELLI: What was his name? It must be loved and revered everywhere.

SOCRATES: Benito Mussolini.

MACHIAVELLI: Do we have an audience? I distinctly heard the sound as of thousands of breaths drawn in suddenly—in reverence, no doubt.

SOCRATES: Ah—

MACHIAVELLI: And now I hear soft laughter from a thousand throats. I will not be laughed at!

SOCRATES: Alas, this is a part of *fortuna* that your *virtù* has not mastered. We are indeed surrounded by a great cloud of witnesses, who see and hear us, though you cannot see them but only a fog.

MACHIAVELLI: Where are they?

SOCRATES: Some of them are in Purgatory with you, enduring your ordeal. Some are in Heaven with me, receiving pleasure and instruction as they watch and listen. And some are still on earth, for our words are being written in a book entitled *Socrates Meets Machiavelli*.

MACHIAVELLI: So since we are not our real selves, but characters in the fiction of some would-be creator, you have not refuted the real Machiavelli.

SOCRATES: This would-be creator is indeed writing fiction, but he is also trying to let us be our real selves.

MACHIAVELLI: Then I demand to be allowed to speak for myself instead of being subjected to your cross-examination!

SOCRATES: And that was precisely the author's plan for you now: the time has come for you to tell your story and explain your philosophy, not by logic and argument, which is my way, but by personal experience, which is yours.

MACHIAVELLI: Well, it's about time! I—

SOCRATES: Excuse me, but I forgot to tell you there are time constraints. You may tell only a ten-minute story.

MACHIAVELLI: But you said there are no time constraints here!

SOCRATES: No, but there are on earth. Most readers there will tire of you after ten minutes. So please tell us only the experiences that shaped your thoughts the most, especially the central thought that all men are bad.

MACHIAVELLI: Hmph! Well, I must play the cards I have been dealt. I see I must still confess being in the same condition I was in when I wrote *The Prince*—the condition that I described in the last sentence of my dedicatory letter to Lorenzo: **"And if your Magnificence, high up at the summit as you are, should occasionally glance down into these deep valleys, you will see I have to put up with the unrelenting malevolence of undeserved ill fortune."**

Wootton, p. 6, ll. 16–19.

SOCRATES: We now know two things: that you are in love with your own words and a whiner. If you lived in America in the twenty-first century you would be a Red Sox fan. No, don't ask; you have wasted a minute already and have only nine left.

MACHIAVELLI: Then I shall narrate the eight main events that have taught me my reluctant but realistic wisdom.

The first is the Pazzi Conspiracy. In 1478 the Pazzi family, who bankrolled the papacy, murdered the true Lorenzo the Magnificent, grandson of *pater patrine* [the father of his country], Cosmo de' Medici, during the Easter Mass in the cathedral, on the signal of the priest's elevation of the Sacred Host. To avenge this sacrilege, the saintly folk of Pisa laid hands on the archbishop of Pisa, who was part of the conspiracy, bound him with a rope around his neck, and threw him out the window of the palace, in full bishop's regalia, together with his Pazzi co-conspirator. The crowd jeered and cheered as the two dangling men bit into each other's flesh, while the other conspirators had all their limbs torn off by the crowd—the crowd of ordinary people. This taught me what lies in wait in the human heart, for if the beast were not in the bush it could not suddenly spring forth into the plain.

Second, in 1494 my beloved city of Florence was humiliated by being occupied by the French king Charles VIII. I saw him march through our streets. This taught me the great difference between being humiliated and humiliating others, between ignominy and glory.

Third, I have already mentioned the instructive interlude of Savonarola, who after four years of being adored and obeyed as a saint and a prophet, and establishing a so-called "Christian Republic", was burned at the stake by his disciples. I saw the flames—and the flames in the eyes and hearts of the people.

Fourth, the most instructive and fascinating man I ever knew was Cesare Borgia. His father had become pope in 1492 by *buying* the office. Not only were most bishops and even popes not celibate in my time, but they often had many mistresses quite publicly, as well as children. Lucrezia Borgia, his sister, entertained with orgies at the Vatican and was most famous and successful at poisoning her enemies. No one knew whether the father of Lucrezia's little bastard boy was her father the pope or Cesare, her brother. Cesare's brother Ivan had been the pope's favorite, so Cesare remedied the problem by murdering him. You see, Cesare was capable of *anything*. He was not an ordinary man; he did not have a conscience.

However, after Cesare's father died, the next pope twice arrested and imprisoned Cesare, and he twice escaped but never regained his power. I resolved to find the causes of such spectacular success and failure.

Fifth, in 1512 the pope's armies surrounded my city, and the citizens refused to fight his Spanish mercenaries. They punished me for supporting Soderini instead of Giuliano de' Medici. They stripped me of my office—I had been a diplomat and negotiator with France and Germany—and bankrupted me and banished me from the city. Four months later I was put in prison because someone put my name on a list of twenty citizens who opposed Giuliano, and one of the twenty was proved to be plotting to assassinate him. I was tortured by the *strappado*—I do not have time to describe it, but it is excruciating—but I survived, was released, and confined to my country estate—a peaceful place whose boring natural beauties I found simply unendurable.

Sixth, I had to curry the favor of the Medici to return to the real life of power and plots. So I wrote my masterpiece, *The Prince*, all in the summer of 1513, distilling all my wisdom, experience, and study of history. It was not appreciated.

Seventh, my opportunity arose when Lorenzo de' Medici died, in 1519, and his successor, Cardinal Giulio de Medici, did employ me as the official historian of the city of Florence. I wrote my *Florentine History* without offending the Medici—a remarkable achievement, as you would realize if you knew this family.

Eighth, in 1527 the citizens of Florence rose against the Medici. I thought I would be restored to their favor, since I had suffered torture, imprisonment, disgrace, and exile for having opposed this family; but the citizens now rejected me for being the *friend* of the Medici cardinal who had become Pope Clement VII. My betrayal by my beloved fellow Florentines put me into despair, then illness, then death. The last date I knew on earth was 1527, when I was fifty-eight years old.

Surrounded by such men in such times, what other conclusions could I have possibly come to than that both man and God, if there is a God, are hopelessly wicked? What practical man could believe in human reason and goodness, or in the power of human reason to make an "ideal state" like Plato's? Or in a Church that spoke the words of righteousness and peace with forked tongue?

SOCRATES: Actually, there is a direct and literal answer to your question. I know two very practical, even cynical men of your time who did exactly that. Though they experienced the same data as you, they drew a different conclusion. One was St. Thomas More, who wrote his *Utopia* just three years after you wrote *The Prince*. He was as much involved with politics and intrigue as you, serving an English tyrant who was as volatile as any Italian. He served loyally as chancellor of England, and he was imprisoned and beheaded. Yet he wrote of an "ideal state" of justice based on natural reason.

MACHIAVELLI: He must have been a simpleton.

SOCRATES: He was a saint.

MACHIAVELLI: I rest my case. He could not have written such a book if he had been an Italian, at any rate.

SOCRATES: But my other example from history *is* an Italian: Boccaccio, a man as cynical as you about the clergy, yet one who drew a different conclusion from the events you experienced. In one of his stories in the *Decameron*, a practical Jewish businessman, Abraham, is contemplating conversion and baptism, at the gentle leading of the pious archbishop of Paris, but has to reside at Rome for a season to do business with the Borgia family and the papal bankers. The archbishop asks him if he wouldn't like to receive baptism before his trip, but he is a practical man, and business must come first. The bishop is convinced that Abraham will never join the Church once he sees her corruptions with his own eyes; but when he returns to Paris, he asks to be baptized! He explains to the startled archbishop, "I'm a practical Jewish businessman. I don't know theology, but I know business. And one thing I know with certainty is that no earthly business that corrupt and venal could possibly last fourteen weeks; this one has lasted over fourteen centuries. It's a miracle! Count me in!"

The point is humorous, even cynical. But it is also serious and even scientific data for argument.

But our time is up, since our readers' patience is ending. Thank you, Niccolò, for your candid and revealing data; our readers will no doubt draw very varied conclusions from it for life as well as for thought. They may even conclude that (to quote the English saint Thomas More) "the times are never so bad but that a good man can live in them."

MACHIAVELLI: Such times I know; such men I do not.

SOCRATES: Not yet, perhaps.

16

The Formula for Success

SOCRATES: We must conclude our investigation of your book by exploring its philosophical conclusion, in chapter 25, **"How Much Fortune Can Achieve in Human Affairs, and How It Is to Be Resisted"**.

First, you part company with Stoic resignation and fatalism—

MACHIAVELLI: To which I was tempted, but I rejected it as naïve optimism's error.

SOCRATES: That is a good example of the virtue of moderation, or the "golden mean" applied to thought.

MACHIAVELLI: Perhaps we are not so far apart as it seems.

SOCRATES: That is often the case after exaggerations and simplifications and stereotypes are overcome. But not always. There is also a golden mean between golden means and extremes.

Now, finally, concerning success and whether we may hope for it by your wisdom, you write:

I am not unaware of the fact that many have held and still hold the view that the affairs

of this world are so completely governed by fortune and by God that human prudence is incapable of correcting them, with the consequence that . . . there is no point in trying too hard; one should simply let chance have its way. . . . Sometimes, thinking this matter over, I have been inclined to adopt a version of this view myself. Nevertheless, since our free will must not be eliminated, I think it may be true that fortune determines one half of our actions, but that, even so, she leaves us to control the other half, or thereabouts.

Wootton, p. 74, ll. 21–26, 29–33.

How prudent of you, by the way, to make provision against one contingency of fortune—the chance that the authorities accuse you of atheism—by confessing the name of the God you did not believe in. If my conscience had only allowed *me* to do that at my trial, I could have saved my skin.

MACHIAVELLI: How do you know the reference is not sincere? You cannot read my heart.

SOCRATES: But I can read your mind, if your words reflect it. No one who believed in God as the Church believes would parallel God with fortune.

MACHIAVELLI: Why not?

SOCRATES: What, pray tell, is the fundamental attitude toward God of those who believe?

MACHIAVELLI: Reverence, piety, obedience, naïveté, superstitious fear—I don't know what answer you are looking for.

SOCRATES: Those will do. Now tell me, what is the fundamental attitude toward fortune according to your wisdom and those who believe it.

MACHIAVELLI: It is summarized in this chapter.

SOCRATES: Especially in its concluding paragraph?

MACHIAVELLI: Yes.

SOCRATES: I quote there the words of Old Saint Nick Machiavelli: **"[F]ortune is a lady** [the translation is a euphemism]**. It is necessary, if you want to master her,** [another euphemism] **to beat and strike her."** What four-letter word do you suggest here? It begins with R.

Wootton, p. 76, ll. 39–40.

MACHIAVELLI: I will not blaspheme even by suggestion.

SOCRATES: Oh, but you already did.

MACHIAVELLI: I have always been careful—

SOCRATES: To avoid compromising appearances, yes, according to your own principle that appearances are more important than reality, or "image is everything." But even if that were true on earth (which it is not), and even if it had worked there (which it did not, in the end), this is the place where there are no more appearances, only reality and unvarnished truth.

MACHIAVELLI: Your job is to examine my book, not my heart.

SOCRATES: Between the two, however, lies your mind. And I must complete my investigation of that mass of knotted ropes that is the rigging of the ship that is you.

MACHIAVELLI: Your imagery is improving the longer you speak with me. You know, I could vastly improve your style if you'd give me a chance.

SOCRATES: You are going to be here for a long time, I think.

MACHIAVELLI: Then—

SOCRATES: No! Back to work! You say about fortune:

> **I compare her** [fortune] **to one of those torrential rivers that, when they get angry, break their banks, knock down trees and buildings, strip the soil from one place and deposit it somewhere else. Everyone flees before them, everyone gives way in face of their onrush, nobody can resist them at any point. But although they are so powerful, this does not mean men, when the waters recede, cannot make repairs and build banks and barriers so that, if the waters rise again, either they will be safely kept within the sluices or at least their onrush will not be so unregulated and destructive. The same thing happens with fortune: She demonstrates her power where precautions have not been taken to resist her.**

Wootton, p. 74, ll. 33–40, p. 75, ll. 1–3.

MACHIAVELLI: Now there's a memorable and fitting image for you, don't you think?

SOCRATES: I do, indeed. But let us see now what traits of character your prince needs to have to conquer this river, or strumpet, or goddess Fortune.

Wootton, p.
75, ll. 19–22.

[A] ruler will flourish if he adjusts his policies as the character of the times changes; and similarly, a ruler will fail if he follows policies that do not correspond to the needs of the times.

MACHIAVELLI: Well?

SOCRATES: Do you see no self-contradiction there?

MACHIAVELLI: Indeed not. Where?

SOCRATES: Your formula for success is the conquest of *fortuna* by your own *virtù*, your powers of mind, will, and arms, is it not?

MACHIAVELLI: Yes.

SOCRATES: And now at the end you finally let the cat out of the bag: In order to be this triumphant, ruthless conqueror, what must you do? You must tailor yourself, your *virtù*, your very character to the winds of Fortune, following her wherever she leads you like a dog.

MACHIAVELLI: That is only a technique, not my supreme formula for success.

SOCRATES: But it is your ultimate explanation of success as you describe it here. For you go on to ask why men of similar character attain different degrees of success, and why men of different character attain similar success, if the formula for success is simply the triumph of *virtù* over *fortuna*. And your answer is that in each case the successful prince does not impose his character upon Fortune but obeys and follows her.

MACHIAVELLI: Do you think *that* is what I meant?

SOCRATES: It is what you say. Here are your words:

> **For we see men, in those activities that carry
> them towards the goal they all share, which is
> the acquisition of glory and riches, proceed
> differently. One acts with caution, while an-
> other is headstrong; one is violent, while
> another relies on skill; one is patient, while
> another is the opposite: And any one of them,
> despite the differences in their methods, may
> achieve his objective. One also sees that of
> two cautious men, one will succeed, and the
> other not; and similarly we see that two men
> can be equally successful though quite differ-
> ent in their behavior, one of them being cau-
> tious and the other headstrong.** [So you, as a
> scientist, naturally seek out the common formula
> that explains all this diverse data. And here it is:]
> **This happens solely because of the character
> of the times, which either suits or is at odds
> with their way of proceeding. . . . But if one
> knew how to change one's character as times
> and circumstances change, one's luck would
> never change.**

Wootton, p. 75, ll. 22–32, p. 76, ll. 5–7.

So your dashing, virile superman turns out to be a dog, a lackey, a wimp! He is a jelly, and Fortune dictates the mold he must fill.

MACHIAVELLI: But he succeeds! The end justifies the means; even if he must use these low means, he attains his high end.

SOCRATES: Does he? Is he now a lord or a servant? Is his *virtù* Fortune's master or slave? Does he even have his own *virtù*?

MACHIAVELLI: What are you saying, Socrates?

SOCRATES: Only what the most practical man who ever lived said: "What does it profit a man if he gain the whole world but lose his own self?" I think I have never heard a more practical sentence than that one.

MACHIAVELLI: But what does it mean?

SOCRATES: You don't know?

MACHIAVELLI: No.

SOCRATES: And you call your thought practical?

MACHIAVELLI: If I accept your insults and name-calling, may I go away?

SOCRATES: No, for I have offered you not insults but arguments. You cannot escape them forever.

But since you accuse me of personal insult, I may as well commit the crime you accuse me of. I will call you a name, Niccolò, and I will also call your philosophy by that name. And I will prove my insult by quoting your whole concluding paragraph:

> **I conclude, then, since fortune changes, and men stubbornly continue to behave in the same way, men flourish when their behavior suits the times and fail when they are out of step. I do think, however, that it is better to be headstrong than cautious, for fortune is a lady. It is necessary, if you want to master her, to beat and strike her. And one sees she more**

often submits to those who act boldly than to those who proceed in a calculating fashion. Moreover, since she is a lady, she smiles on the young, for they are less cautious, more ruthless, and overcome her with their boldness.

Wootton, p. 76, ll. 36–40, p. 77, ll. 1–4.

If you should ever hear a certain song from a time long after yours, sung by a singer rather like yourself—a man named Mick Jagger—I think you will feel very much at home with it. It is called "Always a Woman to Me", and it is a celebration of every evil, lie, and cruelty in a woman, and of the kind of man who would prefer her kind of woman.

The name I must call you, Niccolò, is the name that must be worn by any man whose central dream of success is summarized in the imagery of rape. I call you coward.

MACHIAVELLI: Cur! I challenge you to a duel to the death to defend my honor! Bring us swords!

SOCRATES: We have already had the duel; there are no swords; here you have no honor to defend, and we are both already dead.

MACHIAVELLI: This is intolerable!

SOCRATES: Like death itself? But that is fortune's last trump, and one reason why no man can prevail over her in the end. As you yourself noted in your book —here, in chapter 7—

He told me himself, on the day Julius II was elected, that he had asked himself what he would do if his father died and had been con-

Wootton, p.
26, ll. 26–30.

fident he could handle the situation, but that it had never occurred to him that when his father died he himself would be at death's door.

A famous psychologist of a later century—that man named Freud—discovered that no man can dream or imagine his own death, and therefore we all find it surprisingly difficult to admit the only absolutely certain fact of our life: that "I will die." And you, I think, would have much more difficulty than most, since you cannot admit final defeat to Fortune.

But suppose it is not the faceless goddess Fortune but the Heavenly Father who trumps your desperate desires to conquer and even to live? Do you see the difference that would make to your most basic philosophy?

MACHIAVELLI: It would make folly of my formula of *virtù* and *fortuna*.

SOCRATES: No, it would make it possible! If the soul and its *virtù* are immortal, while the whole world of bodily goods, including *fortuna* is not, then *virtù* can trump *fortuna* in the end. It can even trump Fortune's last trump card, death. As a later poet said, "Death, thou shalt die."

MACHIAVELLI: Oh!

SOCRATES: And the afterworld would also validate and give deeper meaning to your insight into man's wickedness (which, by the way is a very valuable correction to the idealism of Plato, as you rightly claimed). You explain man's ingratitude very well, indeed, when you point to the insatiable nature of human desires. (And this is a profound clue to higher things.) As we discussed earlier, you have written:

> **For of men one can, in general, say this: They are ungrateful, fickle, deceptive and deceiving, avoiders of danger, eager to gain. As long as you serve their interests, they are devoted to you. They promise you their blood, their possessions, their lives, and their children, as I said before, so long as you seem to have no need of them. But as soon as you need help, then turn against you.**

Wootton, p. 52, ll. 1–6.

And you explain this datum very profoundly by this principle: **"The desires of men are insatiable. Their nature urges them to desire all things, but fate permits them to enjoy only a few. This results in a permanent state of discontent, and causes them to despise what they possess."**

St. Augustine himself never said it better than that. It is the "restless heart", and there are only two logically possible interpretations of this puzzling datum that all our desires cannot ever be satisfied in this world. One is that there is no explanation at all, that "that's just the way it is", that "it happens." The other is that "a man's reach must exceed his grasp, or what's a Heaven for?" Now which of these seems more scientific?

MACHIAVELLI: Perhaps I was a failure as a man of science after all.

SOCRATES: Perhaps you can be a success as a man after all.